THE ULTIMATE LEADERSHIP TOOLKIT

"The pessimist complains about the wind.
The optimist expects it to change.
The leader adjusts the sails."
John Maxwell

ABOUT THE AUTHOR

Gaurav Jain has held a variety of leadership positions at technology companies such as Adobe Systems and Autodesk Inc.

Gaurav is a prolific writer on platforms such as Medium.com, and writes about topics ranging from leadership, engineering and life in general.

To learn more about Gaurav, visit www.gauravjain.io

THE *ULTIMATE* LEADERSHIP TOOLKIT

50+ FRAMEWORKS ✕ 20+ CATEGORIES

GAURAV JAIN

Published by Gaurav Jain
ISBN: 9798320992389
https://www.gauravjain.io
gaurav@gauravjain.io

Follow the author:
Medium: @gauravjain
X: @gauravjainio
LinkedIn: @gauravjainio

Cover design by Gaurav Jain

Contents

	Page
Introduction	1
Chapter 1 - Vision and Purpose	2
The Golden Circle	3
Big Hairy Ambitious Goal	4
Chapter 2 - Business Strategy	5
Porter's Five Forces	6
BCG Matrix	7
McKinsey's Three Horizons Model	8
Chapter 3 - Business Analysis	9
SWOT Analysis	10
McKinsey 7-S Framework	11
The Balanced Scorecard	12
Chapter 4 - Prioritization	13
Eisenhower Matrix	14
Pareto Principle	15
Impact-Effort Matrix	16
Chapter 5 - Decision Making	17
OODA Loop	18
System 1 and 2 Thinking	19
Cynefin Framework	20

	Page
Chapter 6 - Execution	21
Agile Methodology	22
The 4 Disciplines of Execution	23
Lean Startup	24
Chapter 7 - Process Improvement	25
Six Sigma	26
The Theory of Constraints	27
Chapter 8 - Productivity	28
Mind-boxing	29
Parkinson's Law	30
Chapter 9 - Team Development	31
Stages of Team Development	32
The Five Dysfunctions of a Team	33
Chapter 10 - Organizational Culture	34
Spiral Dynamics Model	35
Psychological Safety	36
Maslow's Hierarchy of Needs	37
Chapter 11 - Storytelling	38
STAR Technique	39
Hero's Journey	40
Aristotle's Rhetoric	41

	Page
Chapter 12 - Giving Feedback	42
SBI Model	43
Radical Candor	44
Feedback Sandwich	45
Chapter 13 - Goal Setting	46
SMART Goals	47
Goodhart's Law	48
OKR Model	49
Chapter 14 - Accountability	50
RACI Matrix	51
DRI Model	52
Chapter 15 - Problem Solving	53
The 5 Whys	54
First Principles Thinking	55
Chapter 16 - Creative Thinking	56
Design Thinking	57
SCAMPER Technique	58
The Six Hats of Critical Thinking	59
Chapter 17 - Change Management	60
ADKAR Model	61

Kotter's 8-Step Change Model   62

Chapter 18 - Risk Management   63

Animals of Risk   64

Risk Assessment Matrix   65

Chapter 19 - Self-Assessment   66

Johari Window   67

Circle of Competence   68

EQ Framework   69

Chapter 20 - Leadership Models   70

Servant Leadership   71

Situational Leadership   72

Chapter 21 - Leadership Development   73

The Leadership Grid   74

McKinsey 9-box Model   75

Introduction

As a leader, you are faced with a variety of situations: *strategic planning, decision-making, prioritization, giving feedback, communication, goal setting,* and the list goes on.

Your task is to devise the best strategy to handle those situations. You need to use *the best tool for the job*.

During my 2+ decades in various leadership positions across companies, I often ran into situations that I didn't quite know how to handle. I struggled to find the right framework or tool, and sometimes resorted to using "quick fix" solutions.

And those years of struggle led me to build the toolkit that I am presenting to you today.

This book contains more than 50 powerful tools and frameworks across more than 20 categories. Regardless of your role or position as a leader, I'm sure you will find the right tool that works in your situation.

How to use this book

This is your leadership toolkit. Keep it handy, refer to it often, and use the tools in your work regularly.

I hope that this book will empower you to take your leadership to the next level, and here's wishing you the very best!

 Sincerely,

Gaurav
Singapore, March 2024

Chapter 1
Vision and Purpose

"Leadership is the capacity to translate vision into reality."
Warren G. Bennis

The Golden Circle

Simon Sinek (*"Start With Why"*)

The Golden Circle is an alternative perspective about why some leaders and organizations have achieved disproportionately more than others. The principle encourages you to 'start with why' for a purpose-driven approach to business, marketing and life.

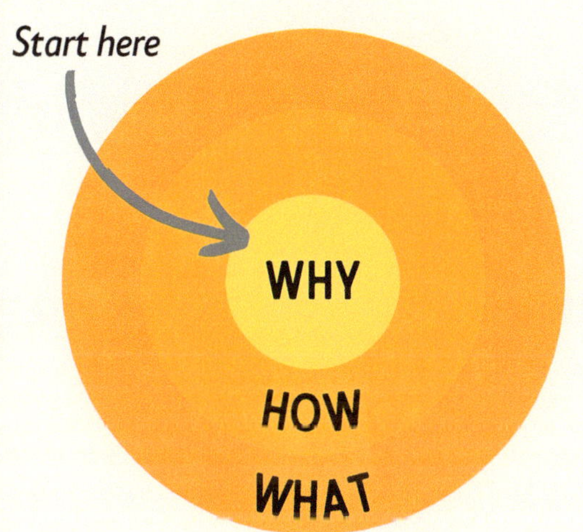

Why
What is the purpose of your existence?

How
What sets you apart from your competition in terms of how you do what you do?

What
What do you do? These could be the products or services you sell.

How it works

Most people and organizations are busy doing what they're doing, but they have no clue Why they do what they do.

The Golden Circle encourages you to ask the most pertinent question before you start any venture or initiative: **Why?**

By asking this question, you identify the core purpose and mission. Once you know the Why, you then move into the How and the What, as they follow naturally from there. You should also continue to realign with the Why and course correct along the way.

Applying the Golden Circle

You can apply the Golden Circle in a variety of situations:

- When you are starting a new project or initiative, identify the *mission* and *vision* before you start defining the roadmap or features.
- When setting a personal or professional goal for yourself, list down the *core purpose* of the goal and *why it matters to you*.
- Don't forget to revisit and *re-align with the Why* as you start working towards a new goal or project

Big Hairy Ambitious Goal

Jim Collins and Jerry Porras (*"Built to Last"*)

BHAG (Big Hairy Audacious Goal) is a visionary concept in leadership where leaders set ambitious, long-term goals that inspire and unite teams, guiding them toward a significant achievement that may seem daunting but ultimately drives successful results.

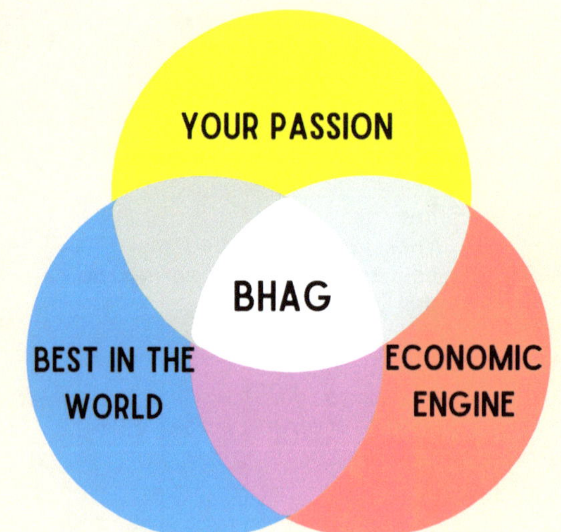

Your Passion
What are you deeply passionate about?

Economic Engine
What drives your economic engine?

Best in the world
What can you be the best in the world at?

How it works

BHAG (Big Hairy Audacious Goal) works by challenging you to set ambitious, long-term objectives that push the boundaries of what seems possible.

BHAGs are an intersection of:
- What your organization is deeply *passionate* about
- What you can be the *best in the world at*
- What drives your *economic engine*

The key is for the goal to be ambitious, inspiring yet still economically relevant and an area that your organization holds expertise in.

Using BHAGs

Here are some examples of popular BHAGs that you can take inspiration from to set your own:

- **SpaceX**: *"Enable human exploration and settlement of Mars"*
- **Meta**: *"Make the world more open and connected"* and *"give everyone the power to share anything with anyone"*
- **Google**: *"Organize the world's information and make it universally accessible and useful"*

Remember to keep the three elements in mind as you set your BHAGs.

Chapter 2

Business Strategy

*"I'm here to build something for the long-term.
Anything else is a distraction."*
Mark Zuckerberg

Porter's Five Forces

Michael E. Porter (*Harvard University*)

Porter's Five Forces is a popular framework to assess competitive dynamics within industries. The framework enables you to make strategic decisions and position your organization to capitalize on opportunities and mitigate threats.

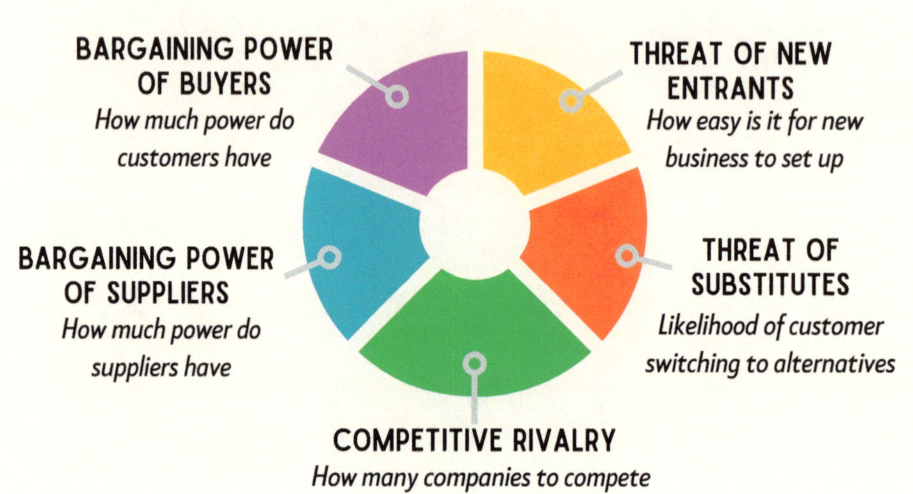

How it works

Porter's Five Forces is a framework assesses 5 aspects:

1. The bargaining power of suppliers
2. The bargaining power of customers
3. The threat of new entrants
4. The threat of substitutes, and
5. The intensity of competitive rivalry

You can utilize this analysis to identify opportunities for growth, anticipate challenges, and develop strategic responses to upcoming opportunities and threats. It provides a holistic approach to strategic decision-making.

Applying the Five Forces

You can apply the Five Forces in a number of situations, including:

- Assess the bargaining power of suppliers and buyers to negotiate favorable terms.
- Analyze the threat of new entrants to anticipate potential competition.
- Evaluate the threat of substitutes to identify risks to existing products or services.
- Understand competitive rivalry to formulate strategies for differentiation and market positioning, including M&A opportunities.

BCG Matrix

Boston Consulting Group

The BCG Matrix provides a strategic framework for analyzing and prioritizing your organization's portfolio of products or services, guiding resource allocation and decision-making for optimal growth and profitability.

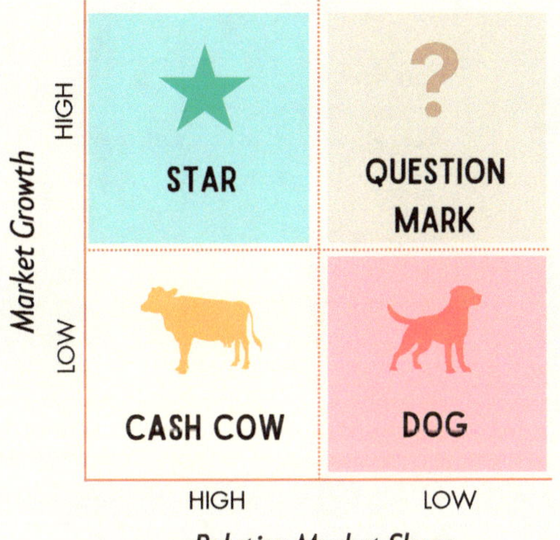

Star
Products that have a high growth rate and a high market share

Question Mark
Products that have a high growth rate but a low market share

Dog
Products that have a low growth rate and a low market share

Cash Cow
Products that have a low growth rate but a high marke share

How it works

The BCG Matrix categorizes products into four quadrants based on market growth rate and relative market share:

1. Stars
2. Cash Cows
3. Question Marks, and
4. Dogs

You can use this analysis to allocate resources effectively, investing in high-growth products (Stars), maximizing profits from established products (Cash Cows), and managing or divesting low-performing products (Question Marks and Dogs).

Applying the BCG Matrix

You can use the BCG matrix in various situations, including:

- Assess your organization's product offerings
- Allocate resources across products/projects based on the matrix's categorization
- Decide which products you want to invest R&D money on (Star), and which ones should be put into maintenance (Cash Cow)

You can apply the BCG matrix during the budget planning cycles.

McKinsey's Three Horizons Model

McKinsey & Company

The McKinsey 3 Horizon Model helps leaders balance short-term goals (Horizon 1), medium-term growth (Horizon 2), and long-term innovation (Horizon 3), ensuring strategic alignment and sustained organizational success across different timeframes.

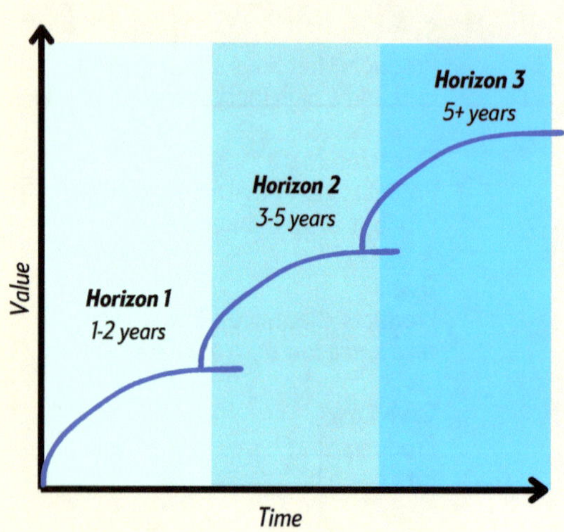

Horizon 1
- 1-2 years
- Defend and expand current core business

Horizon 2
- 3-5 years
- Foster emerging new businesses

Horizon 3
- 5+ years
- Seed future businesses

How it works

The McKinsey Three Horizon model categorizes all initiatives into 3 horizons:

- **Horizon 1**: Focus on optimizing current operations, improving efficiency, and delivering short-term results.
- **Horizon 2**: Explore new opportunities for growth, investing in emerging markets or products to sustain success in the medium term.
- **Horizon 3**: Foster innovation and disruptive ideas, preparing for future industry shifts and maintaining long-term relevance and competitiveness.

Applying the Three Horizons Model

Here are some examples of how you can apply the Three Horizons Model:

- **Horizon 1**: Streamline existing processes, e.g. lean methods in manufacturing to reduce waste
- **Horizon 2**: Invest in R&D for new product lines, like a technology company developing a new software platform
- **Horizon 3**: Start innovation labs to experiment with emerging technologies

The model provide a framework for you to organize and clarify your priorities.

Chapter 3

Business Analysis

"For every leader in the company, not just for me, there are decisions that can be made by analysis. These are the best kinds of decisions."
Jeff Bezos

SWOT Analysis

SWOT analysis is a great tool that leaders can use to take stock of the current situation, and to develop a strategic plan while accounting for competitive opportunities.

Strengths
What are our strengths that we can capitalize on?

Weaknesses
What are our weaknesses that we need to be conscious of?

Opportunities
What are the opportunities that lie ahead?

Threats
What external threats should we be prepared to handle?

How it works

You can apply the SWOT analysis for a specific project or the overall business, and it consists of four elements:
- **Strengths**. These are things your organization does well.
- **Weaknesses**. These are things your organization lacks
- **Opportunities**. These are external opportunities that you can tap into in the future.
- **Threats**. These are external threats that your organization faces.

The idea is to list down each one of those four aspects of your business, and develop a strategy accordingly.

Applying SWOT Analysis

You can take advantage of the SWOT analysis in various ways, including:

- **Strategic Planning**: Do SWOT analysis to identify strengths, weaknesses, opportunities, and threats facing your organization.
- **Product Development**: Evaluate potential product ideas by considering market trends and competitive landscape.
- **Risk Management**: Anticipate risks and plan mitigation strategies.

You can do SWOT analysis during your planning cycle to guide your decisions.

McKinsey 7-S Framework

McKinsey & Company

The McKinsey 7-S Framework is an organizational tool that assesses the well-being and future success of an organization. It looks to seven internal factors as a means of determining whether a company has the structural support to be successful.

Strategy
A well-curated business plan

Structure
How the company is organized

Systems
The business and technical infrastruture

Styles
The management style of the leaders

Staff
Talent management and employees

Skills
Capabilities and competencies

How it works

The McKinsey 7-S framework helps organizations assess and align seven key elements to achieve their goals.

There are two categories of elements
- **Hard elements** that are easily identifiable and influenced by leadership (Strategy, Structure, Systems)
- **Soft elements** that are intagible and culture-driven (Shared Values, Style, Staff, Skills)

All these elements are interconnected and should be aligned to ensure the success of your organization.

Applying the 7-S Framework

You can apply the 7-S Framework to:

- **Diagnose Org Alignment**: Assess how the 7 S's for your teams are aligned with each other and with the overall strategic objectives.
- **Drive Org Changes**: Identify areas you can better align your org to the overall goals. This could involve restructuring, altering processes, or reshaping culture.

You can do this exercise once every year to guide any org changes, make strategic decisions, deliver trainings, etc. for the coming year.

The Balanced Scorecard

The balanced scorecard is a management system aimed at translating an organization's strategic goals into a set of performance objectives that, in turn, are measured, monitored and changed if necessary to ensure that the strategic goals are met.

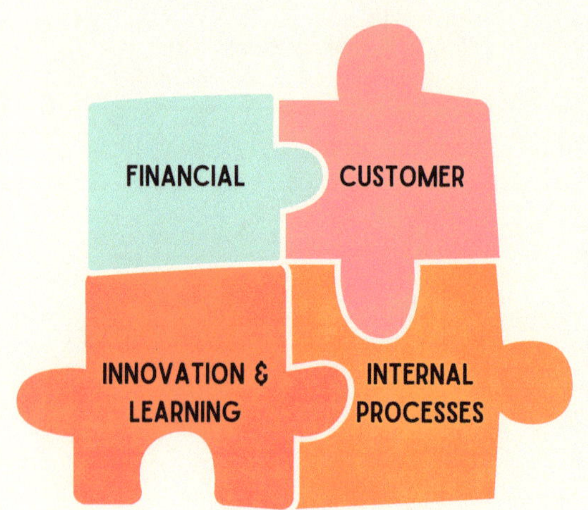

Financial
ROI, Cash Flow, Financial Results

Customer
Customer Satisfaction Rate, Customer Retention, Delivery & Quality

Internal Processes
Cycle time, Engineering Efficiency, Technology capability

Innovation & Learning
Technology leadership, Time to market, Process time to maturity

How it works

The Balanced Scorecard enables you to translate your organization's vision into actionable objectives across four dimensions:

- *financial*,
- *customer*,
- *internal process*, and
- **innovation/learning**

It serves as a comprehensive tool for strategic management, helping you to monitor progress and make informed decisions to drive sustainable success.

Using this method you have a "balanced scorecard" for your organization.

Applying the Balanced Scorecard

You can apply the Balanced Scorecard in various ways:

1. **Setting Strategic Objectives**: Define strategic objectives across financial, customer, internal processes, and learning/growth perspectives.
2. **Aligning Goals**: Ensure alignment of departmental and individual goals with the organization's overall strategy.
3. **Communication**: Use the Balanced Scorecard to communicate strategic priorities and performance expectations to employees at all levels.

Chapter 4

Prioritization

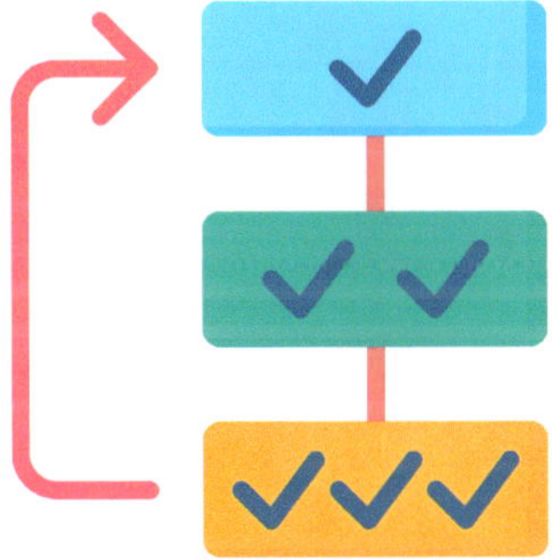

"When you have too many top priorities, you effectively have no top priorities."
Stephen Covey

Eisenhower Matrix

Dwight D. Eisenhower (*former US President*)

The Eisenhower Matrix is a technique that can be used to prioritize tasks that are strategically important and will have the highest return on investment for the business.

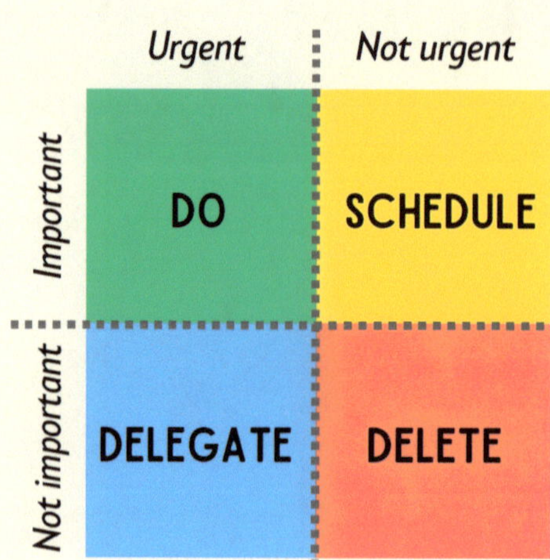

Do
Tasks that are both urgent and important should be done right away

Schedule
Tasks that are strategically important for the long-term should be prioritized

Delegate
Tasks that are urgent but not important should be delegated

Delete
Tasks that are neither urgent nor important should be removed

How it works

Plot your tasks or projects into the *Urgency* vs *Importance* matrix.

- Tasks that are urgent and important should be taken up at the highest priority
- Tasks that are important but not urgent should be scheduled to be picked up soon
- Tasks that are urgent but not strategically important should be delegated
- Tasks that are neither urgent nor important should be removed from the backlog or deferred permanently

Applying the Eisenhower Matrix

You can apply the Eisenhower Matrix in a number of situations, including:

- Identifying the most urgent and pressing priorities for your team at the beginning of a fiscal year
- Deciding on which tasks you should focus on yourself versus delegating to you team
- Create a short list of tasks or projects that you should be investing your energies on

This is a simple yet powerful tool that you can apply in any situation to filter out what needs urgent attention.

Pareto Principle

Vilfredo Pareto (*Italian economist*)

As a leader you would typically have more work than you have the capacity to invest your time on. The Pareto Principle can be used as a smart tool to cut out the noise, and maximize the returns through *ruthless prioritization*.

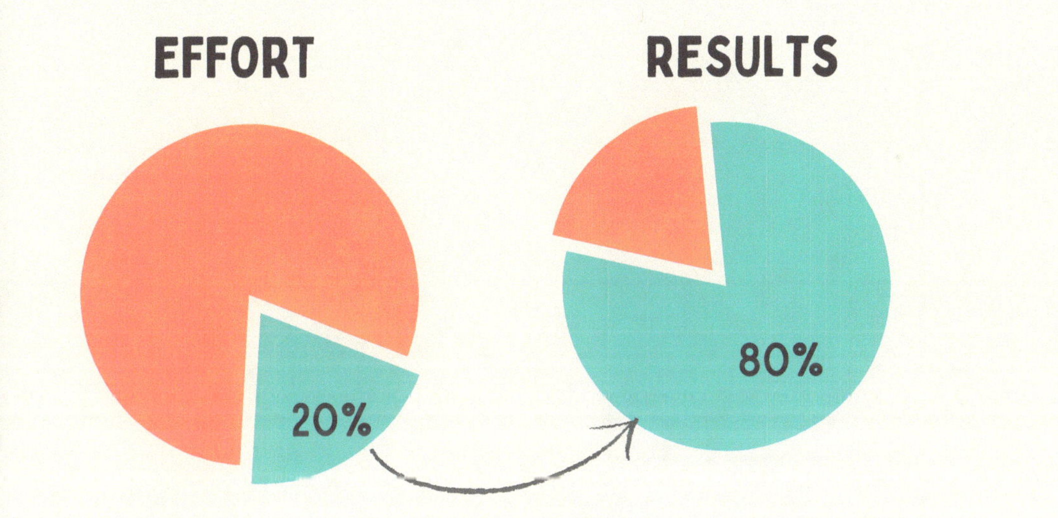

How it works

At its core, the Pareto Principle, sometimes called the 80/20 rule, states that for many outcomes, roughly 80% of consequences come from 20% of the causes.

Another way to put it is that 20% of your projects will yield 80% of the results, or 20% of your team will create 80% of the impact.

This principle forces you to think hard about what your priorities are, and where you should be focusing your attention.

Applying the Pareto Principle

You can apply the Pareto Principle in a variety of situations, including:

- Prioritization of your key projects (by picking just the top 20% of all projects)
- Focusing your energies on the core 20% of the root causes of an incident to maximize the returns on the overall incident
- Disproportionately rewarding the top 20% performers on your team as compared to the remaining members

Impact-Effort Matrix

The Impact-Effort matrix is a simple tool that leaders can use to prioritize their projects and differentiate between strategically important projects and money pits that they should avoid.

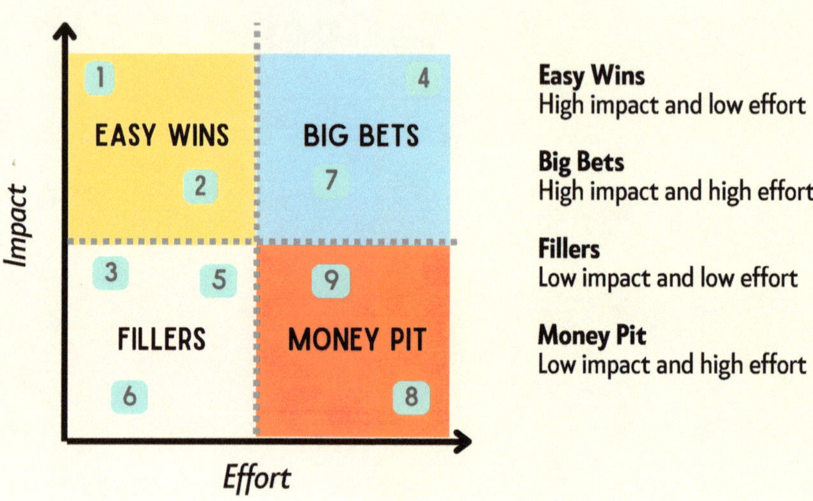

Easy Wins
High impact and low effort

Big Bets
High impact and high effort

Fillers
Low impact and low effort

Money Pit
Low impact and high effort

How it works

Plot your tasks or projects into the *Impact* vs *Effort* matrix.

- Tasks that have high impact and low effort are the low-hanging fruits. These should be picked up first
- Tasks that have high impact and high effort are strategically important and should be scheduled soon
- Tasks that have a low impact and low effort should be considered as "fillers" that can be picked up if and when time is available
- Tasks that have low impact but high effort drain your money and resources, and should be deferred

Applying the Impact-Effort matrix

You can apply the Impact-Effort matrix in a variety of situations, including:

- Differentiating between the big bets and the money pits by articulating the impact and ROI of the large effort projects
- Reassessing the priority and sequencing of projects when are faced with competing priorities
- Reviewing your resource allocations across projects and determining where you want to put your money
- Using the Impact-Effort matrix as a data-point to support a prioritization or deferral decision

Chapter 5

Decision-making

"*Leadership isn't making all the decisions. It is making sure the right decisions are made.*"
Andy Stanley

OODA Loop

John Boyd (*US Air Force Colonel*)

As leaders, we make decisions daily, and these decisions shape the course of our organization. The OODA loop is a simple tool that you can use to improve the quality of decisions made.

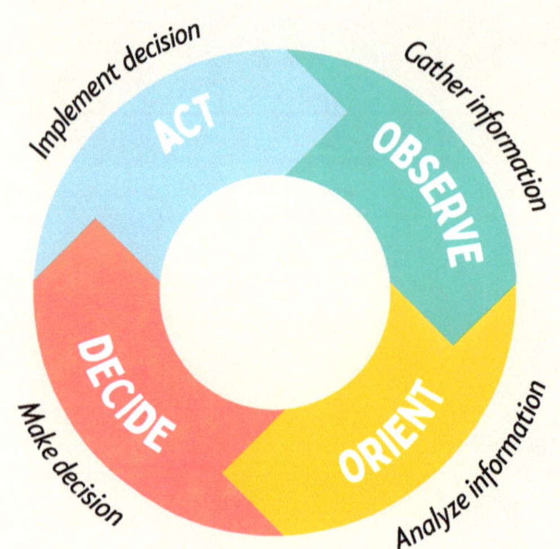

Observe
Collect inputs from as many sources as possible

Orient
Analyze the information that was gathered

Decide
Use the outcome of the analysis to determine the course of action

Act
Implement the decision that was made

How it works

The OODA Loop is a four-point decision model that supports quick, effective, and proactive decision-making. The loop has four stages:
- Observe
- Orient
- Decide, and
- Act

And then there is the ***loop***.

After you implement the decision, you should go back and observe the outcome of the decision, and make any course corrections to ensure an impactful decision.

Applying the OODA Loop

You can apply the OODA loop in any decision-making scenario, including:

- Decisions about prioritization, where the priority may change based on the outcome of execution
- Decisions about user experience, where you can iterate and continue to learn from your beta customers
- Decisions related to people and resource assignments, where you can adjust the allocations

Remember to follow the 4 steps, and the loop, to ensure high-quality, data-driven decisions.

System 1 and 2 Thinking

Daniel Kahneman (*"Thinking Fast and Slow"*)

System 1 and 2 thinking is a behavioral science explanation of how the human brain makes decisions. Being conscious and aware of the triggers and differences in these two systems can help us to make better quality decisions.

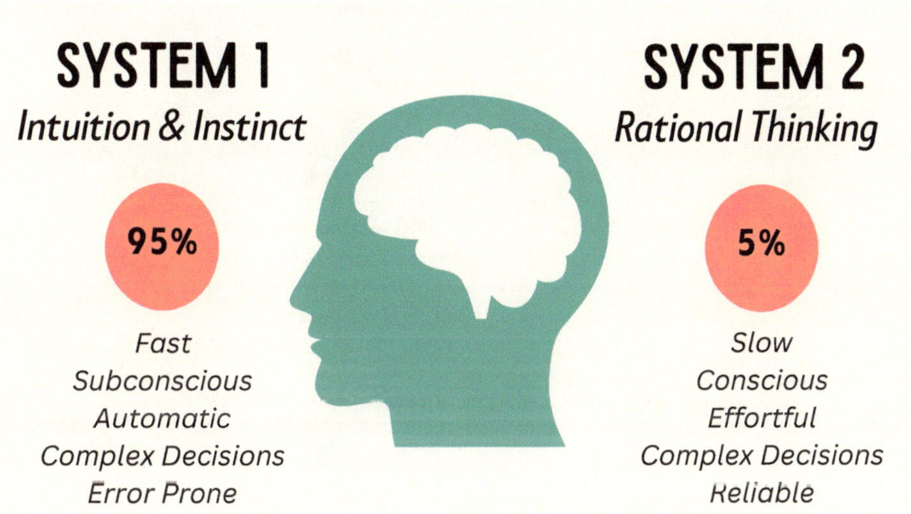

How it works

Our brain has two operating systems - **System 1** and **System 2.**

System 1 thinking:
- Is fast
- Is automatic, unconscious, effortless
- Is driven by intuition
- Does 95% of our thinking

System 2 thinking:
- Is slow
- Is deliberate, conscious, effortful
- Is driven by logic and control
- Does 5% of all our thinking

Applying System 1/2 Thinking

You can use the power of System 1 and 2 thinking by:

- Recognizing the context, and understanding when each mode of thinking is appropriate.
- Being mindful of biases (System 1 thinking is prone to biases and can lead to errors in judgement)
- Slowing down, especially for key decisions that have strategic significance

Doing this consciously and repeatedly will improve the overall decision quality and effectiveness.

Cynefin Framework

David J. Snowden

The Cynefin framework aims to help leaders appreciate that every situation is different and requires a unique approach to decision-making. Based on five "domains", it helps leaders to assess the situation more accurately and respond appropriately.

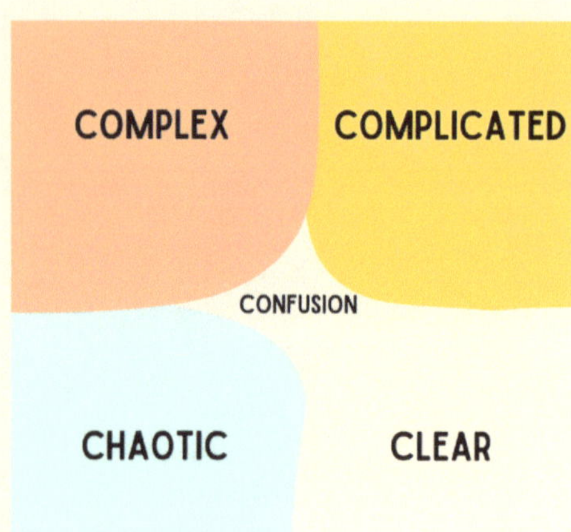

Complex
- Loosely coupled
- probe-sense-respond

Complicated
- Tightly coupled
- sense-analyze-respond

Chaotic
- De-coupled
- act-sense-respond

Clear
- Tightly constrained
- sense-categorize-respond

How it works

The 5 domains are:
- **Clear**. The options are clear and the decision-making approach is "Sense - Categorize - Respond"
- **Complicated**. There are multiple possible solutions, and the decision-making approach to follow is "Sense - Analyze - Respond"
- **Complex**. The probelm is unpredictable, and the best approach to decision-making is "Probe - Sense - Respond"
- **Chaotic**. There is a crisis or emergency, and the decision-making approach is "Act - Sense - Respond"
- **Confusion**. Everything else.

Applying the Cynefin Framework

You can apply the Cynefin framework in any business problem.

The steps to follow are:
- First, and foremost, categorize the problem into one of the 5 domains as per the definitions. For example, if it is a crisis situation, it is a 'Chaotic' problem, and if the solution is obvious, it is 'Clear'
- Use the recommended decision-making steps for the specific problem domain. For example, for Clear problems, you should assess the situation, categorize its type, and respond with the best practices.

Chapter 6

Execution

"Vision without execution is hallucination."
Thomas Edison

Agile Methodology

Ken Schwaber and Jeff Sutherland

Agile was born to address the rigidity of traditional project management process, known as 'waterfall'. Unlike waterfall, Agile promotes a continuous feedback loop with opportunity for rapid prototyping and experimentation.

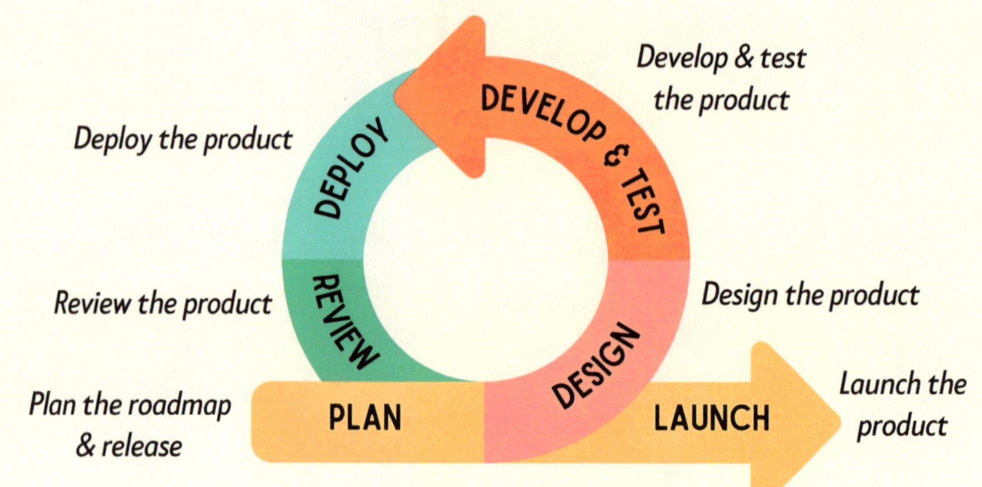

How it works

There are several steps in an Agile process:

- **Plan**. Put together a plan with the target scope and outcomes, looking only at the initial thin slice first.
- **Design**. Design what needs to be developed.
- **Develop & Test**. This is where you develop and test the product or feature
- **Deploy**. Deploy the feature to the customers for feedback.
- **Review**. Incorporate feedback and continue to iterate in the loop until your customer is satisfied.

Applying Agile methodology

Three of the most popular implementations of Agile methodology in use today are:

- **Scrum**. Design your execution in sprints, which are cycles of development
- **Lean**. Inspired by Toyota's lean manufacturing, focused on continuous elimination of waste
- **Kanban**. Organize your tasks to allow for just-in-time adjustments and task execution

You can use the approach that best suits your business needs.

The 4 Disciplines of Execution

Chris McChesney, Sean Covey, Jim Huling (*"The Four Disciplines of Execution"*)

The 4 Disciplines of Execution (4DX) is a simple, repeatable and proven formula for reaching the goals you want to reach as a business or individual. The framework emphasizes on the most important strategic priorities in the midst of urgent activites.

WIGS
Focus on the Wildly Important Goals

Lead Measures
Act on lead measures

Scoreboard
Keep a compelling scoreboard

Accountability
Create a candence of Accountability

How it works

There are 4 essential steps (aka *disciplines*) of the 4DX framework:

1. Focus on **Wildly Important Goals (WIGS)**. Identify the most important goals that need your attention
2. Act on **Lead Measures**, which are activities that drive the success of the WIG
3. Keep compelling **scoreboards** which help you to track progress
4. Create **accountability** by holding frequent meetings that focus on WIGs, reviews, achievements and impediments

Applying 4DX

You can apply the 4 Disciplines of Execution to strategic projects that require your and your team's attention and focus.

You can use 4DX to:
- Drive structured, focused execution of key projects to ensure high transparency and visibility into the progress
- Use the lead measures and scoreboards to make data-driven decisions to help keep the project on track

Lean Startup

Eric Ries (*"The Lean Startup"*)

Lean startup is a methodology for developing businesses and products that aims to shorten product development cycles and rapidly discover if a proposed business model is viable by adopting the Build/Measure/Learn cycle.

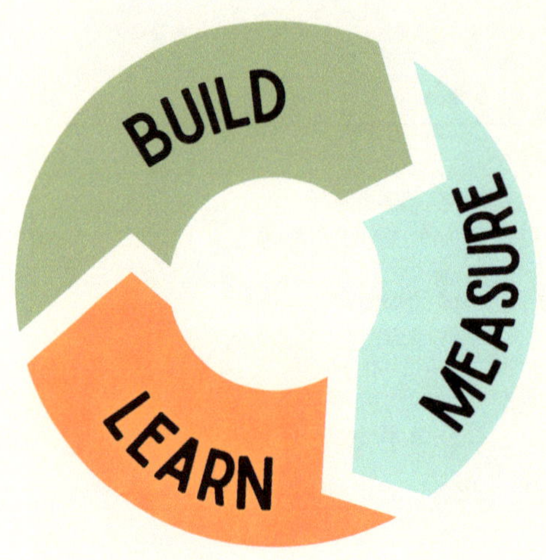

Build
Build/refine a Minimum Viable Product

Measure
Measure customer reaction

Learn
Learn & innovate while developing a legal customer base

How it works

The Lean Startup provides a scientific approach to creating and managing new initiatives and getting the desired product into the customer's hands faster.

- **Build** - In this phase you build a Minimum Viable Product (MVP) that is enough to deploy to a customer
- **Measure** - In this phase you get feedback from your customers on the MVP that was delivered
- **Learn** - In this phase you incorporate the feedback, and continue to build the legal customer base.

Applying the Lean Startup

You can apply the Lean Startup methodology in a number of situations:

- Testing a new idea or concept as a potential base for a new / emerging startup
- Starting a new product idea or feature within a large organization
- Iterating on improvements to an existing product with the help of an existing customer base

The philosophy is as critical as the implementation. Make sure to have the right processes in place that aid Build/Measure/Learn philosophy.

Process Improvement

"Continuous improvement is better than delayed perfection."
Mark Twain

Six Sigma

Bill Smith (*Motorola*)

Six Sigma, also sometimes referred to as DMAIC, is a comprehensive quality control methodology focused on reducing defects and improving processes within an organization.

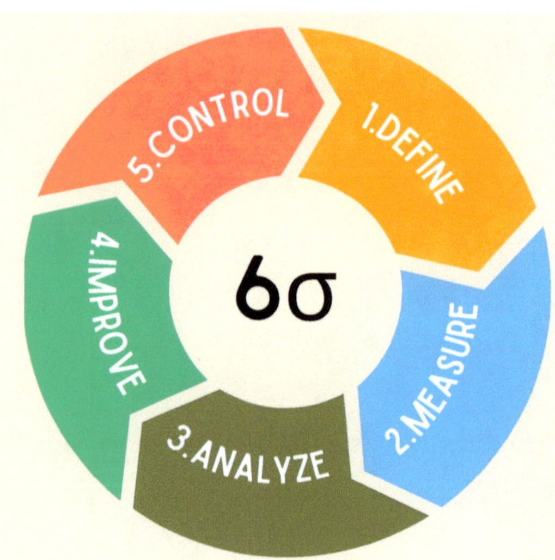

Define
Define the process and the problem

Measure
Measure the current performance

Analyze
Analyze the process for issues and root causes

Improve
Determine and implement improvement actions

Control
Maintain the improved process

How it works

Six Sigma follows a structured approach called DMAIC: *Define, Measure, Analyze, Improve,* and *Control.*

1. **Define**: Identify the problem, project goals, and scope.
2. **Measure**: Quantify the current process performance using data.
3. **Analyze**: Identify root causes of defects or inefficiencies.
4. **Improve**: Develop and implement solutions to address identified issues.
5. **Control**: Establish measures to sustain improvements and ensure stability.

Applying Six Sigma

You can apply Six Sigma in a number of situations:

- **Process Improvement:** You can apply Six Sigma methodology to a specific processes within your organization (e.g., fulfilment) to improve the efficiency
- **Quality Control**: You can use Six Sigma to establish quality standards, develop metrics and improve overall quality of products
- **Cost Reduction**: You can use Six Sigma to identify opportunities for cost reduction by eliminating waste, reducing defects and optimizing specific processes.

The Theory of Constraints

Eliyahu M. Goldratt (*"The Goal"*)

The Theory of Constraints is a process improvement methodology that emphasizes the importance of identifying the "system constraint" or bottleneck that stands in the way of achieving a goal.

Identify
Identify the constraint or bottleneck

Exploit
Maximize the utilization of the constraint

Subordinate
Align all other processes in the system to support the constraint

Elevate
Invest in increasing its capacity

Repeat
Repeat the process with the next constraint

How it works

The Theory of Constraints operates on the premise that *every system has at least one constraint that limits its ability to achieve its goals.*

The theory suggests a five-step process, which involves identifying the constraint (bottleneck), maximizing it's utilization, aligning all other activities to the constraint, increasing the capacity of the constraint, and then repeating the entire process for the next constraint.

This process ensures that the weakest link is addressed first, as it yields the maximum returns.

Applying the Theory of Constraints

You can apply the Theory of Constraints in a variety of situations:

- **Process Improvement:** By focusing on improving or eliminating constraints, you can enhance productivity, reduce cycle times, and improve quality of any process in your system.
- **Project Management:** By ensuring that the constraints are adequately addressed and managed, you can minimize delays and improve project outcomes

Chapter 8
Productivity

"Productivity is less about what you do with your time, and more about how you run your mind."
Robin S. Sharma

Mind-boxing

Gaurav Jain

Time is the scarcest resource, and mind-boxing is a simple framework that leaders — regardless of level or role — can use to be more intentional about how they spend their time. The idea is to maximize the impact by *scheduling your priorities*.

	PEOPLE	PROCESS	PRODUCT
STRATEGY	20%	20%	30%
TACTICS	10%	10%	10%

The 3 Ps (Verticals):

- **People**: ensuring the well-being of your team
- **Process**: driving operational efficiency
- **Product**: delighting your customers with a great product, platform or service

The 2 Layers:

- **Tactics**: delivering results, getting the job done
- **Strategy**: driving long-term strategy

How it works

Mind-boxing operates by categorizing a leader's role into 6 distinct boxes, which are formed by the intersection of the 3 verticals (or 3 Ps) and the 2 layers.

The three verticals (or P's) - the **People**, **Process**, and **Product** - form your core responsibilities.

The two layers - **Strategy** and **Tactics** - define the level at which you operate.

Your goal is to allocate time to each of the 6 boxes (adding up to a total of 100%), and then align all your work to match those numbers.

Applying Mind-boxing

You can apply the framework in 3 steps:

- Decide how you want to allocate your time between the 6 boxes based on your goals and priorities. Note that the total should add up to 100%.
- Review your calendar, your TODO lists, and any other planning tool you use, and align those with your 6-box time allocation.
- On a regular basis (say, once per month), review your time allocation and adjust it based on changing priorities, roles or business needs.

Parkinson's Law

Cyril Northcote Parkinson (*The Economist*)

Parkinsons's Law is an adage that states that *"Work expands so as to fill the time available for its completion."* While not a scientific principle, it has been tested to be true as it closely follows the human tendency to procrastinate.

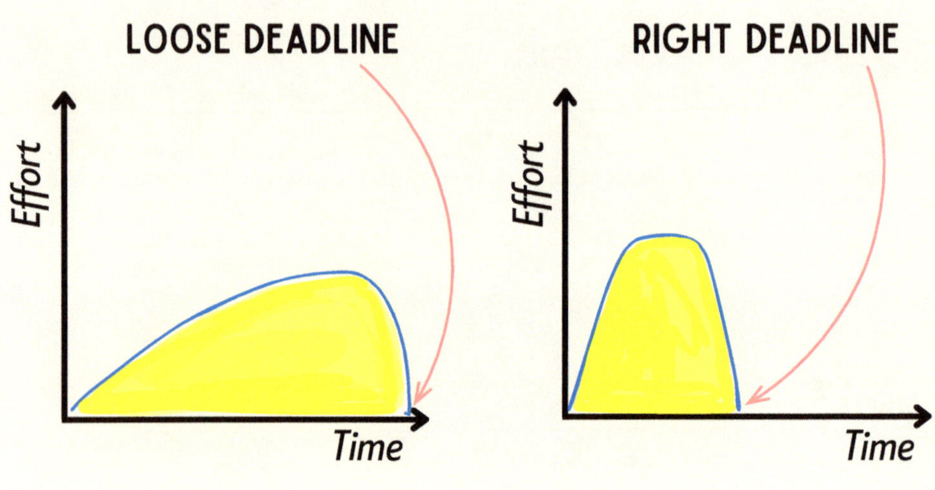

How it works

At its core, the principle is very simple. The longer you set a deadline for a given task, the more work you will end up doing to accomplish it.

Parkinson's law can also lead people to procrastinate, leaving tasks until right before they are due.

This expansion means that the task becomes even more daunting, requiring more mental energy. The 'extra time' that that task requires is often related to the mental stress caused by worrying about getting it done, and not the task itself.

Applying the Parkinson's Law

You can apply the Parkinson's Law in a number of situations:

- **Setting deadlines**. You should set *stretch goals* and *realistic deadlines*. These will force teams to prioritize effectively and avoid procrastination or delays.
- **Promoting efficiency**. You can promote efficient execution and discourage long-running tasks by keeping the law in mind.
- **Encouraging work-life balance**. By discouraging procrastination, you can allow your team members to set boundaries between work and life.

Chapter 9

Team Development

"Coming together is a beginning. Keeping together is progress. Working together is success."
Henry Ford

Stages of Team Development

Bruce W. Tuckman

Bruce Tuckman, an educational psychologist, identified a five-stage development process that most teams follow to become high performing. This model can be used to better prepare and set up teams for success as they navigate these stages.

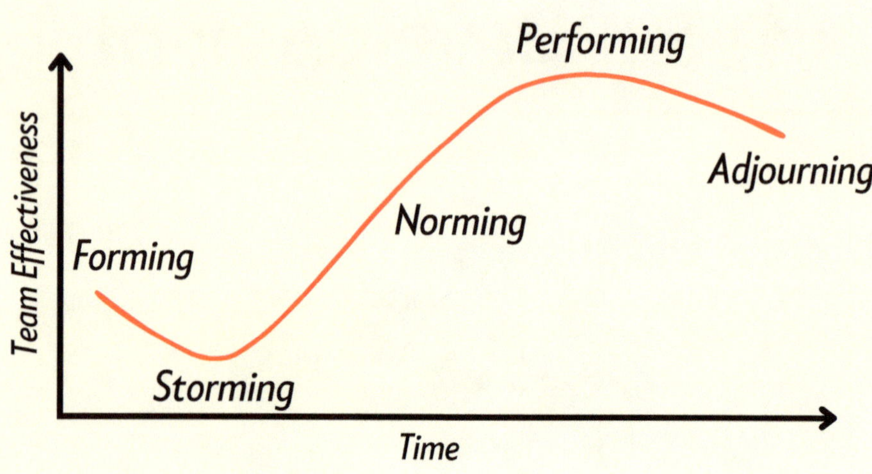

How it works

Tuckman's stages of team development include:

1. **Forming**: Initially, teams form and acquaint themselves with tasks.
2. This is followed by the **storming** phase, where conflicts arise as members establish their roles.
3. **Norming** occurs as consensus is reached, and cooperation improves.
4. During **performing**, the team operates efficiently, and goals are achieved.
5. Finally, **adjourning** involves the dissolution of the team upon completion of the task.

Applying Tuckman's Model

You can apply Tuckman's model by guiding your teams through the stages:

- During the forming stage, you can facilitate introductions and clarify goals
- In the storming phase, you can mediate conflicts constructively
- As the team moves into the norming stage, you can reinforce positive behaviors and establish norms for communication
- Finally, during the performing stage, you can empower team members to take ownership of their tasks while providing support

The Five Dysfunctions of a Team

Patrick Lencioni (*"The Five Dysfunctions of a Team"*)

The Five Dysfunctions of a Team, as introduced by Patrick Lencioni, are the pitfalls that teams face as they seek to "grow together". According to Lencioni, these dysfunctions are the fundamental causes of organizational politics and team failure.

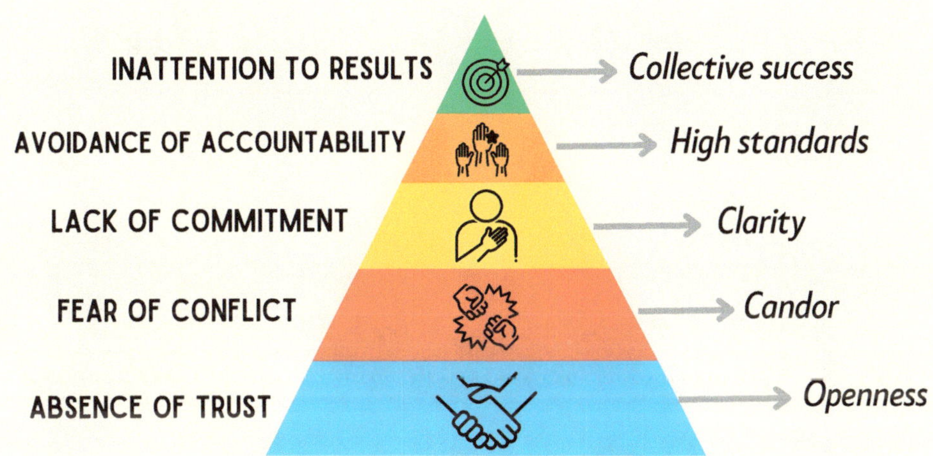

How it works

You must address the *five dysfunctions* to build a strong team.

- By fostering **trust** through *vulnerability* and *authenticity*, you encourage open communication.
- You can ensure **commitment** by clarifying *goals* and *expectations*, while holding team members *accountable* for their roles. This ensures that everyone is aligned and focused on achieving results.
- Ultimately, by addressing these dysfunctions, you can create an environment where teams thrive, and *collectively succeed*.

Applying the Five Dysfunctions

You can apply the learnings from the Five Dysfunctions of a Team by:

- Encouraging open discussions during team meetings
- Welcoming diverse perspectives and constructive conflicts
- Setting clear goals and expectations, and ensure commitment
- Holding regular accountability check-in meetings, and track progress towards the goals
- Having regular feedback discussions for 2-way feedback to promote trust and collaboration

Chapter 10

Organizational Culture

"If you get the culture right, most of the other stuff will just take care of itself."
Tony Hsieh

Spiral Dynamics Model

Prof. Clare W. Graves (*Union College, New York*)

Spiral Dynamics is a developmental model that helps leaders understand diverse values and perspectives within their organizations, guiding them to adapt leadership strategies to foster growth, inclusivity, and resilience.

Holistic: Inspire collective purpose

Integrative: Use Systems thinking

Community: Encourage collaboration

Success: Drive innovation and results

Order: Ensure adherence to norms

Power: Lead with power and confidence

Security: Provide safety & harmony

Survival: Meet basic needs of team

How it works

Spiral Dynamics maps the evolving developmental stages of individuals, teams, and organizations, ranging from *survival instincts* to *holistic awareness*.

You can leverage this model to understand cultural dynamics, tailor communication strategies, navigate change, foster inclusive environments, and promote growth.

By recognizing and respecting the diversity of values and perspectives, you can effectively manage teams, drive innovation, and cultivate resilient organizations.

Applying the Spiral Dynamics Model

You can utilize the Spiral Dynamics model in several ways:

1. **Cultural Assessment**: You can assess your organization's culture to understand the prevailing values, beliefs, and behaviors.
2. **Talent Management**: You can form your team development and training initiatives based on inputs from the model.

You can use the model to build awareness around your organization, and use that to form strategies for the future development and growth.

Psychological Safety

Carl Rogers (*later popularized by Amy Edmondson*)

Psychological safety, a term coined by Carl Rogers and later popularized by Amy Admendson, refers to the freedom to speak freely and take risks without fear of retaliation by management or those in positions of power.

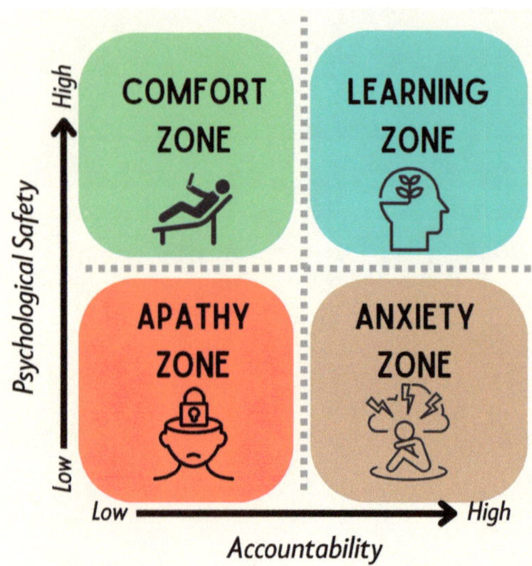

Comfort Zone
High psychological safety but low accountability. *Too easy.*

Apathy Zone
Low psychological safety and low accountability. *Ignored.*

Anxiety Zone
High Accountability but low psychological safety. *Stressful.*

Learning Zone
The right level of accountability and psychological safety. *Challenged.*

How it works

Psychological safety fosters an environment where team members feel comfortable taking risks and expressing themselves without fear of judgment.

On the other hand, **accountability** ensures that individuals take responsibility for their actions and commitments, crucial for achieving goals and maintaining trust.

As an effective leader you *balance both*: nurturing psychological safety to empower your teams while maintaining accountability to ensure productivity and drive towards business results.

Applying Psychological Safety

Examples of how you can apply Psychological Safety:
- You can hold regular team meetings where everyone feels free to voice opinions or concerns without fear of criticism. You can be transparent and authentic to encourage open communication.
- While doing so, you should also set clear guidelines, deadlines, and responsibilities for tasks.

The key is to balance psychological safety and accountability, and aim to move your team towards the 'Learning Zone".

Maslow's Hierarchy of Needs

Abraham Maslow ("*A Theory of Human Motivation*")

In 1943 psychologist Abraham Maslow coined the idea of *The Hierarchy of Human Needs*, and how human motivation and behavior can be mapped to these needs. Leadership, much like human development, can be understood through the lens of Maslow's Hierarchy of Needs.

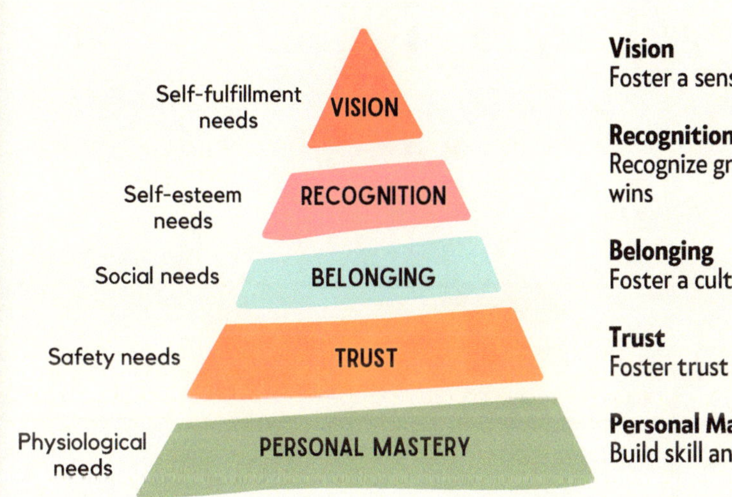

Vision
Foster a sense of purpose

Recognition
Recognize great work and celebrate wins

Belonging
Foster a culture of belonging

Trust
Foster trust and psychological safety

Personal Mastery
Build skill and expertise in the field

How it works

At the very bottom of the hierarchy we start with meeting the *physiological* and *safety* needs, which translate into building expertise in our field, and fostering trust in the team.

As we climb up the hierarchy, we have the *social* and *self-esteem* needs, which translate into fostering belonging and recognition in the team.

Finally, at the peak of the hierarchy is the need for *self-fulfilment*, which we can satisfy by fostering a sense of purpose and mission.

Applying Maslow's Hierarchy of Needs

You can apply Maslow's Hierarchy of Needs in your context in a number of ways:

- You can address basic physiological and safety needs by providing fair compensation and a safe work environment.
- You can fulfil social & esteem needs by fostering a sense of belonging and rewarding individual contributions
- Finally, you can provide opportunities for personal and professional growth, empowering teams to reach their full potential.

Storytelling

"Storytelling is the most powerful way to put ideas into the world today."
Robert McAfee Brown

STAR Technique

At the core of communication lies a very important skill — *storytelling*. The STAR framework can be used to create impactful stories, which can help with negotiations, influence, and could mean the difference between failed and successful projects.

How it works

The STAR framework has 4 steps:

1. **Situation**. This is where you set the stage for the story.
2. **Task**. This is the task that needs to be performed, or the problem that needs to be solved.
3. **Action**. This is the action that you or your team performed.
4. **Result**. This is the outcome of the action you took, and should directly address the task or problem you described.

You must follow the steps in order, and keep buildong on the previous step.

Applying the STAR Technique

You can apply the STAR Technique in a variety of situations, including:

- Sharing the justification for your team member's promotion at a calibration meeting by sharing specific examples and anecdotes
- Making a pitch to your boss for an opportunity that you think you deserve based on your past accomplishments by emphasizing your accomplishments
- Responding to behavioral interviews with compelling stories that highlight what you bring to the table

Hero's Journey

Joseph Campbell

The Hero's Journey provides a powerful narrative framework that helps engage and inspire audiences, conveying leadership lessons, values, and visions in a compelling and relatable manner.

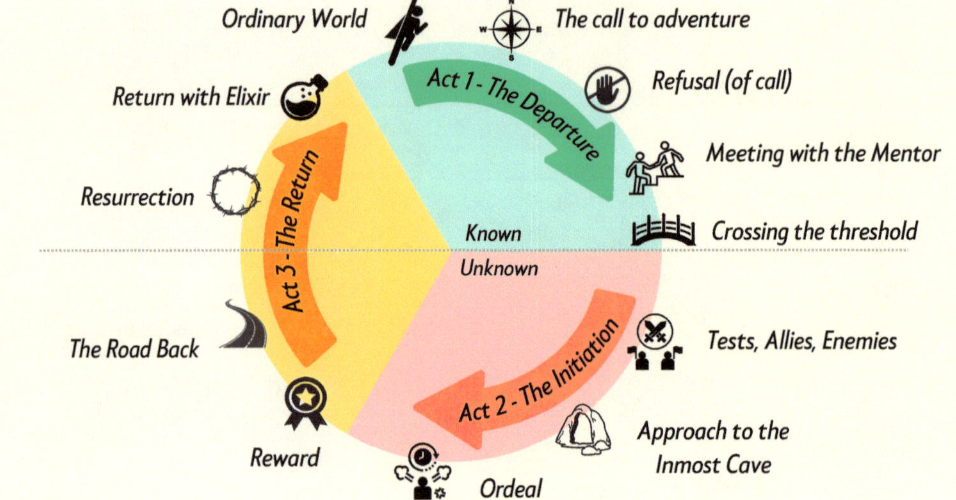

How it works

The Hero's Journey framework for storytelling follows a protagonist through stages of *adventure*, *challenges*, and *growth*. This is a popular method used in the context of book and film story design.

In the context of leaders, this framework allows leaders to craft narratives that resonate with audiences, illustrating personal and professional challenges, triumphs, and transformations.

The framework allows you to inspire and engage your audience with relatable experiences and leadership lessons.

Applying the Hero's Journey

You can apply the Hero's Journey framework by:

- Sharing your personal anecdotes of overcoming challenges and achieving success.
- Crafting narratives that illustrate leadership principles, values, and vision.
- Using storytelling in team meetings, presentations, or company events to inspire and motivate employees.
- Encouraging employees to share their own Hero's Journey stories, fostering a culture of resilience, growth, and empowerment.

Aristotle's Rhetoric

Aristotle

Aristotle's rhetoric provides a foundation for effective persuasion, enabling leaders to communicate with clarity, credibility, and emotional appeal, thereby influencing and inspiring others towards shared goals and visions.

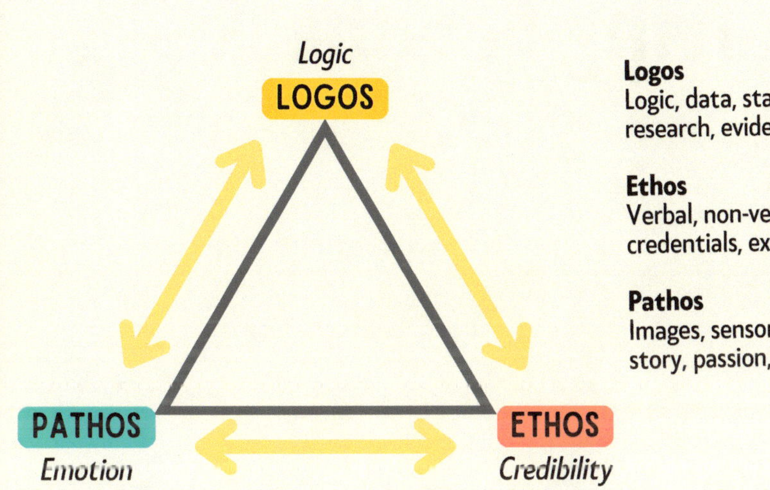

Logos
Logic, data, statistics, research, evidence

Ethos
Verbal, non-verbal, values, credentials, experience

Pathos
Images, sensory language, story, passion, purpose

How it works

Aristotle's rhetoric for persuasion involves three key components:

- **Ethos** (credibility)
- **Pathos** (emotional appeal)
- **Logos** (logical reasoning)

This framework helps establish credibility by demonstrating expertise and integrity, appeals to emotions to inspire action, and employs logical arguments to persuade and influence stakeholders effectively.

Effectively, the framework is a great tool for building persuasive arguments.

Applying Aristotle's Rhetoric

You can apply Aristotle's rhetoric by:

- Emphasizing ethos through demonstrating expertise and integrity in your communication to your teams and stakeholders
- Utilizing pathos by appealing to employees' emotions, such as pride in their work or a sense of purpose.
- Employing logos by presenting logical arguments and data to support decisions and initiatives, enhancing credibility and persuasiveness.

Chapter 12

Giving Feedback

*"We all need people who will give us feedback.
That's how we improve."*
Bill Gates

SBI Model

The SBI model provides a simple and effective framework that leaders can use to deliver high-impact feedback. The model encourages objectivity, transparency, and empathy, all at the same time.

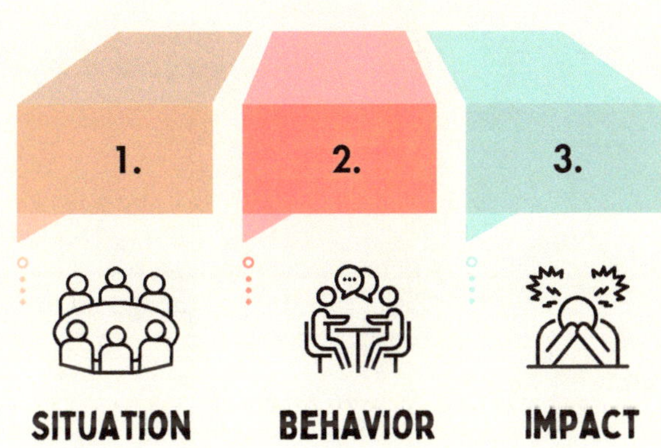

Situation:
Set the context (Who, When, Where)

Behavior:
What happened (Actions, Behaviors)

Impact:
What was the impact (Results, Outcome)

How it works

When delivering feedback, follow this 3 step model:

- **Situation**. First, describe the situation or context. Who was involved? When did it happen? Where did it happen?
- **Behavior**. Second, share the actual behavior that was observed. Avoid labelling or generalizing.
- **Impact**. Finally, share the impact or outcomes of the behavior.

The core idea is to stay away from labelling individuals, and stick to observed behavior and objective data.

Applying the SBI Model

You can apply the SBI model in a variety of situations, including:

- Sharing positive or constructive feedback with your team members (you should do this soon after the situation for higher impact)
- Sharing feedback with your peer, colleague, or even your boss (this could be positive or constructive feedback)
- Reflecting on your own behavior or sharing that with your boss or your team members

Radical Candor

Kim Malone Scott ("*Radical Candor*")

Radical candor, a term coined by Kim Scott, encourages leaders to be brutally honest when giving feedback, while not losing sight of humanity. The feedback delivered through this approach is both kind and clear, specific and sincere.

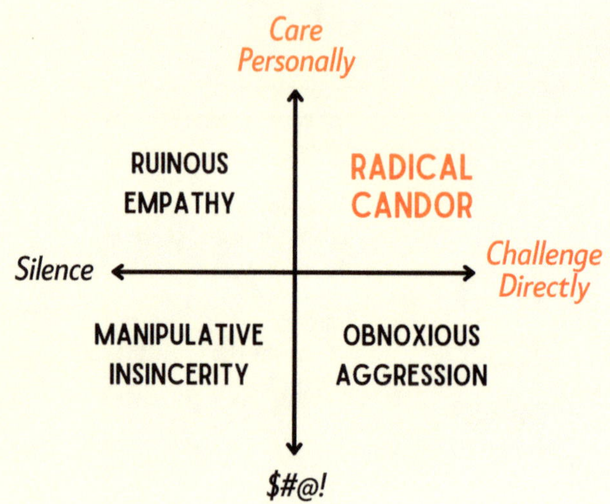

Radical Candor
Being honest, empathic, and direct when delivering feedback

Obnoxious Aggression
Criticizing and publicly embarrassing without any care

Manipulative Insincerity
Being fake and not caring about the other person

Ruinous Empathy
Sugarcoating and diluting the message, undermining the feedback

How it works

Radical candor involves leaders providing *honest* feedback while *caring personally* about their team members.

It encourages direct communication, addressing issues *openly* and *constructively*.

Leaders offer both praise and criticism, as needed, promoting growth and development. This direct and empathic approach to delivering feedback encourages trust and transparency, ultimately helping to improve the results in the organization.

Applying Radical Candor

You can apply radical candor in a number of situations, including:

- Schedule regular one-on-one meetings with your team members, and offer specific praise for a job well done and constructive criticism for areas needing improvement
- Encourage open dialogue during team meetings, allowing everyone to voice their opinions and concerns without fear of retribution.
- Lead by example by being transparent about your own challenges and mistakes, promoting a culture of honesty

Feedback Sandwich

Mary Kay Ash (*Mary Kay Cosmetics*)

The feedback sandwich method helps leaders deliver constructive criticism effectively by sandwiching it between positive feedback. This approach maintains motivation, fosters growth, and strengthens relationships between leaders and team members.

How it works

The feedback sandwich method involves delivering constructive criticism by sandwiching it between positive feedback.

1. Leaders start with positive comments to establish rapport and acknowledge strengths.
2. They then provide specific areas for improvement or criticism.
3. Finally, they end on a positive note, reinforcing encouragement and support.

This approach ensures feedback is balanced and constructive.

Applying the Feedback Sandwich

Feedback sandwich should not be used to dilute the feedback, but as a way to keep the team member encouraged to work towards the feedback.

Example:
1. *"I appreciate your contributions on Project A, and your presentation last week was timely."*
2. *"However, in your presentation you could have included A, B and C. I would like you to work on those aspects for future such sessions."*
3. *"Please know that I'm here to offer any support you need in making that happen. Thank you."*

Chapter 13

Goal Setting

> *"Setting goals is the first step in turning the invisible into the visible."*
> **Tony Robbins**

SMART Goals

George T. Doran

SMART goals are crucial for leaders as they ensure clarity, focus, and accountability. By being Specific, Measurable, Achievable, Relevant, and Time-bound, SMART goals help leaders drive performance, track progress, and achieve desired outcomes effectively.

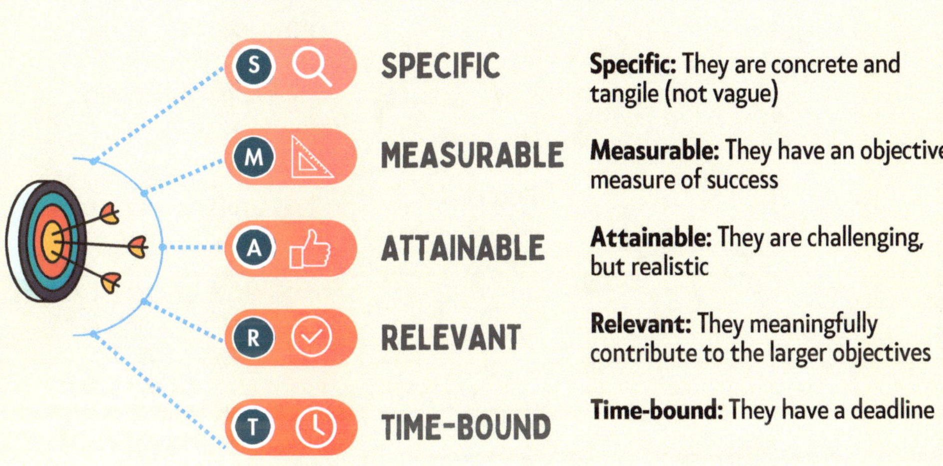

How it works

SMART Goals are:

- **Specific**: Leaders define clear, precise goals, avoiding ambiguity.
- **Measurable**: Goals are quantifiable, allowing leaders to track progress objectively.
- **Achievable**: Leaders set realistic goals within reach of resources and capabilities.
- **Relevant**: Goals align with organizational objectives and contribute to overall success.
- **Time-bound**: Leaders establish deadlines, fostering urgency and ensuring timely completion of goals.

Applying SMART Goals

You can use this framework to improve the quality of goals you set for your organization. An example of SMART goal could be:

"Increasing Sales Revenue":
- Specific: "*Increase quarterly sales revenue by 15%.*"
- Measurable: "*Track sales figures weekly.*"
- Achievable: "*Provide sales team with additional training.*"
- Relevant: "*Align with company's growth strategy.*"
- Time-bound: "*Achieve target within the next three quarters.*"

Goodhart's Law

Charles Goodhart

Goodhart's Law highlights the risk that when a measure becomes a target, it ceases to be a good measure. In leadership, relying solely on metrics can lead to unintended consequences as people may manipulate them to meet targets, compromising true performance and organizational goals.

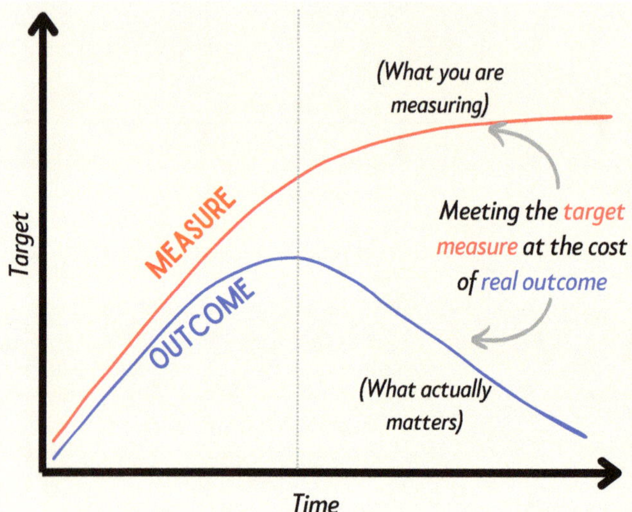

OUTCOME
What actually matters.
Example: *product quality*

METRIC
What you are measuring as a proxy to assess the outcome.
Example: *No. of bugs logged*

In the above example, if you set targets for bug counts logged by your team as a way to measure product quality, you may end up with a large number of bugs logged with no quality improvement

How it works

If you focus solely on achieving specific metrics or targets, you may unintentionally incentivize behaviors that optimize for those metrics at the expense of broader organizational goals.

You can counter Goodhart's law by applying the 2-D formula for your metrics:

- **Define** your metrics clearly and crisply, so there is very little room for misinterpretation
- **Diversify** your metrics so that it is harder for the metrics to skew the results and still lead to the overall goal

Countering Goodhart's Law

Here is an example of how you can diversity your "Sales Target" metric to counter Goldhart's Law:

- Alongside sales targets, you can also measure *customer satisfaction* and *employee engagement*
- Adding customer satisfaction discourages sales team from being overly aggressive. The last thing you want is a high sales revenue at the cost of customer trust.
- Adding employee engagement as a measure discourages unrealistic sales targets that undermine the well-being of the sales teams.

OKR Model

Andrew Grove (*Intel*)

The OKR (Objectives and Key Results) model is vital for leaders as it provides a framework for setting clear, measurable goals and aligning team efforts, fostering focus, accountability, and driving organizational success.

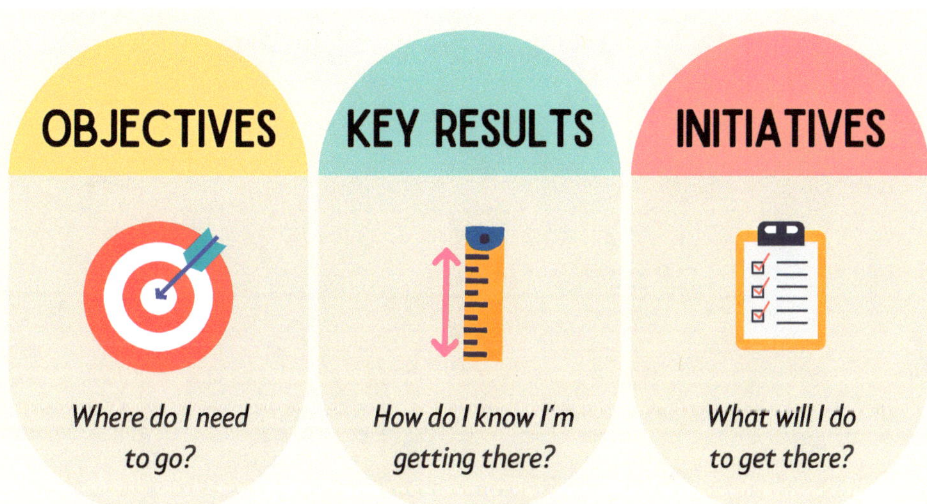

How it works

There are 3 elements of the OKR Model:
- Leaders set clear, ambitious **Objectives**, defining what needs to be achieved.
- **Key Results** are established, measurable outcomes that indicate progress toward the Objectives.
- Teams align their efforts around **initiatives** to achieve these Key Results.

Regular check-ins and progress tracking ensure accountability and allow for adjustments.

Applying the OKR Model

You can apply the OKR model in any situation where they need to set a goal or objective. Examples of applications include:

- Launching a Product: Set Objective: "Successfully launch new product X." Key Results: "Achieve 10,000 pre-orders," "Secure 50 positive media mentions,"
- Improving Employee Engagement: Objective: "Enhance employee satisfaction." Key Results: "Increase employee engagement survey scores by 20%," "Reduce employee turnover rate by 15%,"

Chapter 14

Accountability

"Accountability is the glue that ties commitment to results."
Bob Proctor

RACI Matrix

Edmond F. Sheehan

It is widely believed that *Everybody's responsibility is nobody's responsibility*. The RACI matrix is designed to drive accountability for important projects and initiatives, while ensuring transparency and clarity of communication.

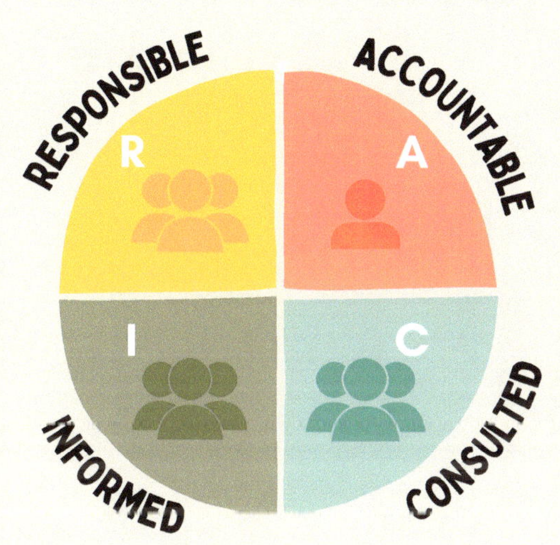

Responsible
Responsible for completing the task (1 or more persons)

Accountable
Accountable for the success of the task (1 person)

Consulted
Consulted during execution of the task (1 or more persons)

Informed
Informed regardin progress of the task (1 or more persons)

How it works

In the RACI matrix, there are 4 key stakeholders: **Responsible**, **Accountable**, **Consulted** and **Informed**.

The idea is to explicitly identify the 4 types of stakeholders. This ensures clarity, transparency and accountability.

Every stakeholder is expected to focus on their role as defined by the RACI matrix, and avoid stepping into other roles.

Leaders use the matrix to ensure accountability, avoiding confusion and promoting efficiency.

Applying the RACI Matrix

The RACI matrix can be applied in a variety of situations, including driving accountability for high-profile projects and enabling smooth flow of communication in complex projects.

As an example, if you are launching a new product, you may have:

- The Marketing team as *Responsible* for the promotional activities
- The Project Manager as *Accountable* for overall coordination
- The Sales team as *Consulted* for customer feedback, and
- The Customer Support team as *Informed* for updates.

DRI Model

Apple, Inc.

The Directly Responsible Individual (DRI) model is a leadership approach where specific individuals are assigned clear ownership and accountability for tasks or projects within a team, streamlining decision-making and ensuring accountability.

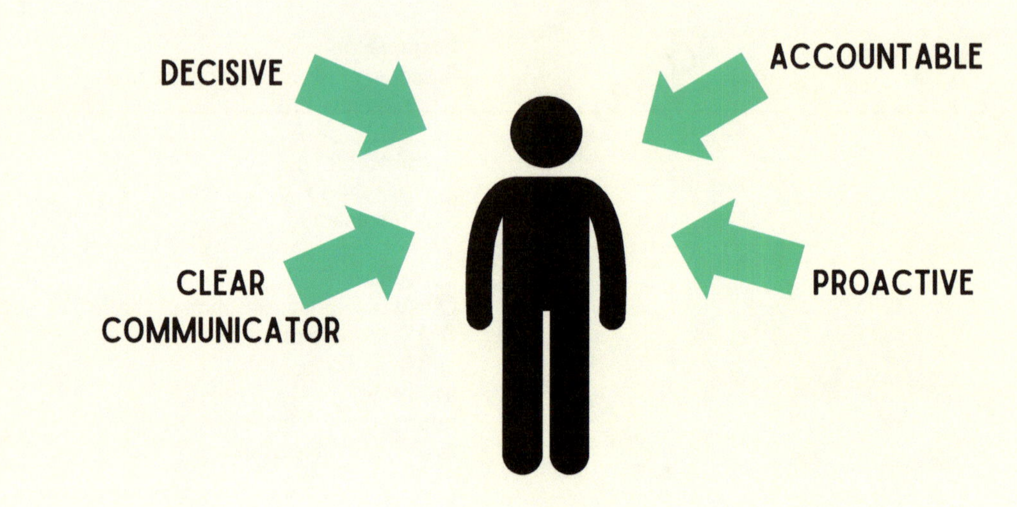

How it works

The DRI model has a few salient features:

- Each task or project is assigned a Directly Responsible Individual (DRI).
- The DRI takes full ownership and accountability for the success of that task or project.
- They are empowered to make decisions and drive progress without unnecessary bureaucracy.
- Clear lines of responsibility streamline communication and ensure efficient execution, enhancing overall team effectiveness and productivity.

Applying the DRI Model

Examples of DRI applications:

- **Product Development:** Assign a DRI for each feature, ensuring clear ownership and accountability. For example, appoint a DRI for user interface design, who coordinates with the design team and provides regular updates to stakeholders.
- **Marketing Campaigns**: Designate a DRI for each campaign, responsible for its planning, execution, and evaluation. For instance, appoint a DRI for a social media campaign, who coordinates content creation, schedules posts, and monitors performance metrics.

Chapter 15

Problem Solving

"*Your ability to solve problems and make good decisions is the true measure of your skill as a leader.*"
Brian Tracy

The 5 Whys

Sakichi Toyoda (*founder of Toyota Industries*)

One aspect of your role as a leader is to solve problems. However, many times you may end up addressing the symptom, not the problem itself. The 5 Why's framework helps to dig deeper into situations like those, and uncover the root causes.

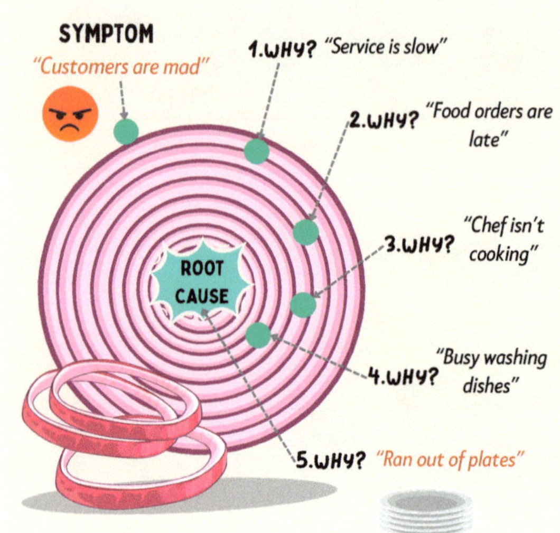

Symptom
What appears to be the problem on the surface

The 5 Whys
Intentional prompts to uncover the deeper cause of the problem

Root Cause
The ultimate source of the problem

How it works

Applying the 5 Whys is like peeling the layers of an onion:

- When you are faced with a problem, do not settle on the initial solution or interpretation.
- Instead, ask Why? and list down the response.
- Repeat this process by asking Why? again, until you end up with the root cause or the essence of the problem.
- Typically, after 5 Whys you should end up with the root cause

Applying the 5 Whys

You can apply the 5 Whys in a number of situations, including:

- Finding the root cause of a problem, including customer issues. You can start by describing the issue, and then asking "Why did that happen?" until you land at the root cause.
- Establishing your organization's vision. You can start by asking: "Why do we do what we do?" If you repeat the 5 Whys, it will lead you to the deeper reason and inspiration for your organization

First Principles Thinking

First principles thinking is a problem-solving technique that can be used to come up with new approaches to solving problems by breaking the problem into its fundamental components.

How it works

In First Principles thinking, you break down a complex problem into fundamental truths or basic principles, and then reconstruct solutions from the ground up.

It follows a 3 step process:
1. **Identify the problem**, and clarify assumptions. This could be anything from designing a product to optimizing a process
2. **Break down the problem** into its fundamental components
3. **Create new solutions** using the building blocks, and don't get constrained by existing solutions.

Applying First Principles thinking

First principles thinking can be applied any problem solving scenario, including:

- Solving a complex problem, such as "designing a more efficient electric car battery"
- Understanding the root cause of a problem, such as "why did the product fail in this scenario?"
- Coming up with innovative and creative solutions to address an unserved need in the market

The key is to follow the 3-step process of identifying the problem, breaking it down, and creating new solutions.

Chapter 16

Creative Thinking

"Creativity is seeing what everyone else has seen, and thinking what no one else has thought."
Albert Einstein

Design Thinking

Design thinking offers a human-centered approach to problem-solving, fostering innovation, empathy, and collaboration. It enables leaders to address complex challenges effectively and create solutions that resonate with stakeholders.

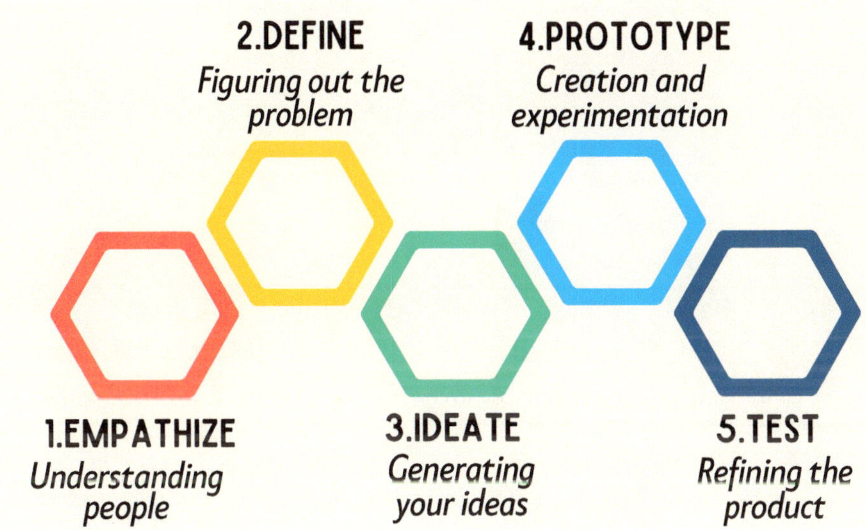

How it works

1. **Empathy**: Leaders immerse themselves in the experiences of stakeholders to understand their needs and perspectives.
2. **Define**: They clearly define the problem or challenge based on insights gathered.
3. **Ideate**: Leaders brainstorm creative solutions without limitations, encouraging diverse perspectives.
4. **Prototype**: They develop and test prototypes to quickly iterate and refine ideas.
5. **Test**: Leaders gather feedback from stakeholders to validate solutions before implementation.

Applying Design Thinking

Examples of usage of design thinking:

- **Product Development:** When creating new products or services, you can apply design thinking to ensure they meet user needs effectively.
- **Process Improvement:** You can use design thinking to streamline workflows and enhance efficiency, focusing on improving your employee experience.
- **Customer Experience**: Design thinking helps you innovate to deliver exceptional customer experiences and increase satisfaction and loyalty.

SCAMPER Technique

Bob Eberle (*"Scamper: Games for Imagination Development"*)

The SCAMPER technique fosters innovation and creativity by providing a structured approach to generating new ideas, improving processes, and solving problems, ultimately driving organizational growth and adaptation.

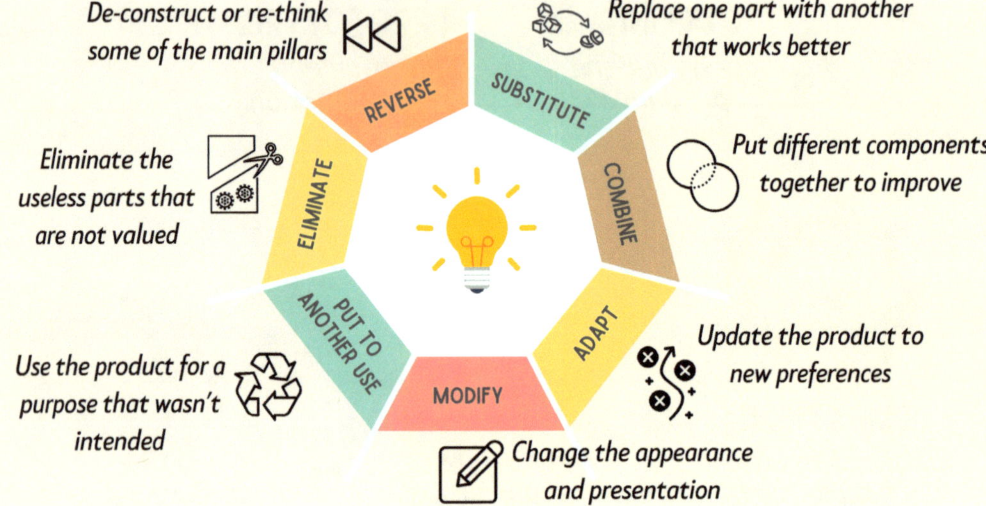

How it works

SCAMPER is a lateral thinking technique which challenges the status quo and helps you explore new possibilities.

The SCAMPER technique aims to provide seven different thinking approaches to find innovative ideas and solutions. These are **Substitute, Combine, Adapt, Modify, Put** to another use, **Eliminate** and **Reverse**.

There is no sequential flow to follow while moving from each of the seven thinking techniques, and any response to the SCAMPER technique is welcomed no matter how non-logical it is.

Applying the SCAMPER Technique

Here is an example usage in a Product Development scenario:

- Substitute: Swap out traditional packaging for eco-friendly materials.
- Combine: Merge product features for a unique offering.
- Adapt: Adjust design to target new demographics.
- Modify: Update specs to match evolving consumer trends.
- Put to another use: Donate excess inventory.
- Eliminate: Streamline design.
- Reverse/Rearrange: Rearrange workflows for efficiency.

The Six Hats of Critical Thinking

Dr. Edward de Bono (*"Six Thinking Hats"*)

The six hats of critical thinking are relevant for leaders as they provide a structured approach to decision-making, fostering comprehensive analysis, creativity, and collaborative problem-solving, ultimately leading to more informed and effective leadership strategies.

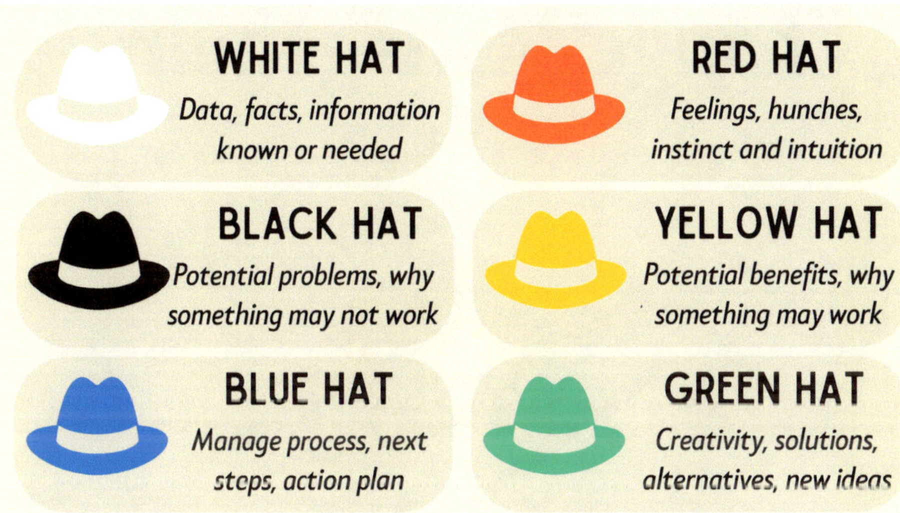

How it works

- **White Hat**: Leaders focus on gathering facts and information objectively.
- **Red Hat**: They express emotions and intuition without justification, considering gut feelings.
- **Black Hat**: Leaders critically analyze potential risks and drawbacks.
- **Yellow Hat**: They explore benefits and opportunities optimistically.
- **Green Hat**: Leaders generate creative ideas and innovative solutions.
- **Blue Hat**: They oversee the thinking process, ensuring all perspectives are considered

Applying the Six Hats

You can apply the Six Hats approach in any situation that requires critical thinking.

As an example, when devising a new business strategy, you can apply the six hats of critical thinking to ensure a comprehensive approach.

You may analyze market data (White Hat), consider team morale (Red Hat), evaluate risks (Black Hat), explore opportunities (Yellow Hat), brainstorm innovative ideas (Green Hat), and oversee the entire process (Blue Hat).

Change Management

"Change is hard at first, messy in the middle, and gorgeous at the end."
Robin Sharma

ADKAR Model

Jeff Hiatt (*founder of Prosci*)

The ADKAR change management model that provides a structured framework to guide individuals through change by focusing on Awareness, Desire, Knowledge, Ability, and Reinforcement, ensuring successful organizational transitions.

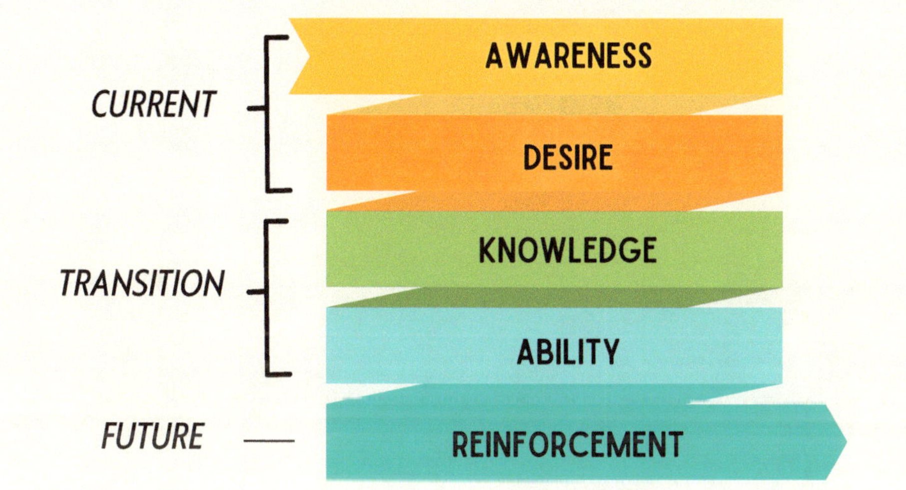

How it works

- **Awareness**: Leaders communicate the need for change and its implications.
- **Desire**: They cultivate motivation and commitment among team members to embrace the change.
- **Knowledge**: Leaders provide the necessary information and resources for individuals to understand how to change.
- **Ability**: They support skill development and provide opportunities for practice.
- **Reinforcement**: Leaders ensure sustained change by recognizing and rewarding desired behaviors.

Applying the ADKAR Model

The ADKAR model can be applied in any change scenario. As an example, when implementing a new technology you can apply the model as follows:

- Awareness: Communicate benefits and reasons for the change.
- Desire: Foster excitement and ownership through incentives.
- Knowledge: Provide training on the new technology.
- Ability: Offer ongoing support and resources for skill development.
- Reinforcement: Recognize and reward early adopters to encourage continued usage.

Kotter's 8-Step Change Model

John Kotter ("*Leading Change*")

The Kotter 8-Step Change Model is a framework for leaders that provides a systematic approach to managing organizational change, ensuring successful implementation through clear communication, engagement, and continuous monitoring of progress.

How it works

The Kotter 8-Step Change Model guides leaders through a systematic process of organizational transformation.

It starts with creating urgency and assembling a coalition to champion change. Leaders articulate a compelling vision, communicate it effectively, and eliminate obstacles hindering progress. By celebrating initial successes, they maintain momentum and gradually embed the change into the organizational culture. Continuous reinforcement ensures the sustainability of the change, ultimately fostering a culture of adaptability.

Applying the Kotter Model

The Kotter model can be applied in any major change scenario. As an example, in case of restructuring operations, you can:

- Create Urgency: Highlight market challenges and the need for agility.
- Form a Powerful Coalition: Gather senior executives to lead the change effort.
- Communicate the Vision: Clearly articulate the new operational model and its benefits.
- Remove Obstacles: Address resistance by providing necessary resources and training.

Chapter 18

Risk Management

"Success is about smart risk management, not about wild risk taking."
Michael Masterson

Animals of Risk

Leaders can use the Animals of Risk as a framework to implement a structured and intentional risk-assessment exercise for their organizations. The framework involves plotting the risks on a Predictability vs Probability matrix, and then associate it with one of the animal metaphors.

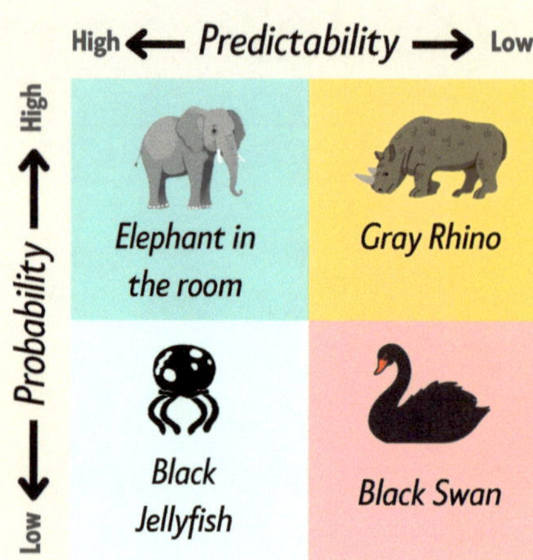

Elephant in the room
Well-known, obvious risk that no-one wants to talk about

Gray Rhino
Highly probable risk that is hard to predict

Black Jellyfish
A risk that has low chances, and is obvious when it is actually faced

Black Swan
Highly improbably events that cannot be predicted

How it works

Animals of risk are metaphors that we can use to help us manage risk and make better business decisions.

- **Elephant in the room** is a problem that is obvious yet nobody wants to talk about it.
- **Black Swans**, which are rare in nature, represent a highly unlikely events that are difficult to predict
- All rhinos are gray, and a **Gray Rhino** represents risks that are likely to happen yet we can't predict them
- A **Black Jellyfish** represents a threat that is highly unlikely, yet after it happens it seems obvious

Applying the Animals of Risk

When faced with a risk or threat, you should plot it in the **Predictability** vs **Probability** matrix as illustrated above, and then ask yourself:

- Which animal does this threat most closely represent based on your plotting?
- If you're looking at a Gray Rhino or a Black Jellyfish, you can explore ways to mitigate the impending risk
- For Elephants in the room, you need to call the obvious and take action
- For Black Swans, there is usually not much you can do other than acknowledge that they exist

Risk Assessment Matrix

US Air Force

The Risk Assessment Matrix, often used by leaders, assesses risks based on their likelihood and potential impact. It aids in decision-making by visually categorizing risks into high, medium, or low priority, enabling effective mitigation strategies.

Impact *of risk* →

Probability of risk ↑	Insignificant 1	Minor 2	Significant 3	Major 4	Severe 5
Almost certain 5	5	10	15	20	25
Likely 4	4	8	12	16	20
Moderate 3	3	6	9	12	15
Unlikely 2	2	4	6	8	10
Rare 1	1	2	3	4	5

VERY LOW	LOW	MEDIUM	HIGH	VERY HIGH	EXTREME

How it works

Risks are categorized into two broad attributes:

- **Impact**, which is the severity of the issue in case the risk occurs. This could range from Insignificant (1) all the way up to Sever (5)
- **Probability**, which is the likelihood of the risk occurring. This ranges from Rare (1) all the way up to Almost Certain (5).

The product of Impact and Probability gives the final risk measure, which ranges from Very Low to Extreme, and leaders can use that to make decision about how to handle the risk.

Applying the Risk Matrix

You can use the Risk Matrix in a variety of situations, including:

- **Project Management:** You can use the risk matrix to assess potential project delays or budget overruns. For instance, you can identify high-impact risks like supply chain disruptions and allocate contingency funds accordingly.
- **Business Expansion:** Before entering new markets, you can analyze risks such as regulatory hurdles or cultural differences using the matrix. You can develop entry strategies tailored to mitigate these risks.

Chapter 19

Self-Awareness

"*Many leadership problems are driven by low self-awareness.*"
Bill Hybels

The Johari Window

Joseph Luft and Harrington Ingham

You can use the Johari Window in your organization to identify your blind spots, build trust, develop self-awareness, and improve understanding and interpersonal relationships with your teams.

	Known to self	Not known to self
Known to others	OPEN AREA	BLIND SPOT
Not known to others	HIDDEN AREA	UNKNOWN

The Open Area
Things known to self and to others.

The Hidden Area
Things known to self and not known to others.

The Blind Spot
Things known to others but not known to self.

The Unknown
Things not known to self, nor to others.

How it works

The Johari Window is split into four quadrants:

- Open Area
- Hidden Area
- Blind Spot
- Unknown

You can identify your Johari window by listing down your own perception of yourself, your style, and strengths, and then comparing notes with someone else you work with. You can then use that to identify your blind spots, and chalk out a plan to address them.

Applying the Johari Window

You can apply the Johari Window in a variety of situations, including:

- Team Building: You can use the Johari Window to facilitate team-building activities, such as sharing personal insights and feedback among team members to improve mutual understanding and collaboration.
- Conflict Resolution: You can apply the Johari Window to help resolve conflicts in the team by uncovering hidden feelings or misunderstandings and promoting open dialogue and empathy.

Circle of Competence

Warren Buffet and Charlie Munger

The circle of competence is crucial for leaders as it enables them to focus on their strengths, make informed decisions, delegate effectively, and ultimately drive organizational success by leveraging expertise where it matters most.

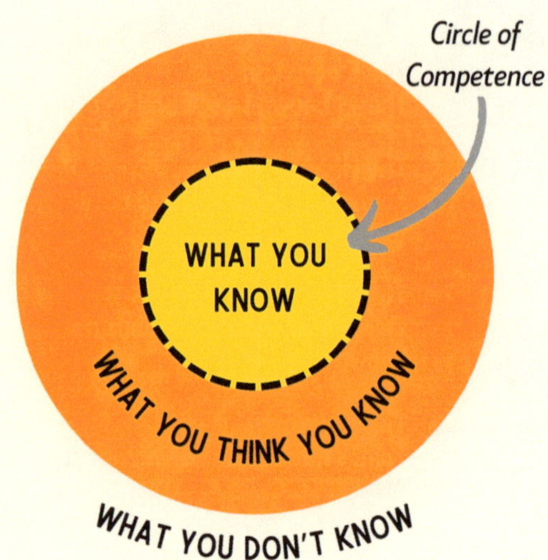

What you know
What you know and that matters to your business and you can control. This forms your *Circle of Competence*

What you think you know
What you don't know and it matters to your business but you can't control

What you don't know
What you don't know and it does not matter for your business and you can't control.

How it works

The circle of competence describes a person's natural competence in an area that matches their skills and abilities.

Effective leaders understand their strengths and limitations within this circle and make decisions accordingly. They focus on leveraging their expertise to guide their teams and organizations toward success, while also recognizing when to seek input or delegate tasks outside their expertise.

The key is to be well aware of your circle of competence, and the boundaries.

Applying the Circle of Comptence

You can apply the circle of competence by aligning tasks and responsibilities with your expertise and strengths.

For example, if you have a background in *marketing* you might focus on developing strategic marketing plans, while delegating financial decisions to a CFO with expertise in finance.

As another example, if you excel in *software development* you might focus on overseeing product development initiatives and driving innovation in software solutions.

EQ Framework

Daniel Goleman (*"Emotional Intelligence"*)

Emotional intelligence (EQ) is vital for leaders as it enables them to understand and manage their own emotions, navigate interpersonal relationships effectively, inspire and motivate others, and foster a positive work environment conducive to productivity and collaboration.

Self-awareness
Emotional self-awareness, self-assessment, self-confidence

Social Awareness
Empathy, organizational awareness, service orientation

Self Management
Self-control, adaptability, achievement drive

Relationship Management
Influence, developing others, teamwork & collaboration

How it works

The EQ framework involves leaders being aware of the 4 quadrants: **Self-awareness, Social awareness, Self-management** and **Relationship management.**

Leaders with high EQ can regulate their emotions in stressful situations, communicate effectively, build strong relationships, and inspire trust and loyalty among team members.

By leveraging EQ skills, leaders can handle different situations strategically and professionally.

Applying the EQ Framework

You can apply the emotional intelligence (EQ) framework in a number of ways, including:

- Cultivating self-awareness through reflection and feedback.
- Practicing self-regulation by managing your emotions effectively in challenging situations, maintaining composure and making rational decisions.
- Demonstrating empathy by actively listening to your team members, understanding their perspectives, and providing support when needed.

Chapter 20

Leadership Models

"*The best leaders don't know just one style of leadership - they're skilled at several, and know how to switch when needed.*"
Daniel Goleman

Servant Leadership

Robert K. Greenleaf (*"The Servant as Leader"*)

Servant leadership prioritizes serving the needs of others, empowering and uplifting individuals, fostering a culture of empathy, collaboration, and growth, ultimately leading to organizational success.

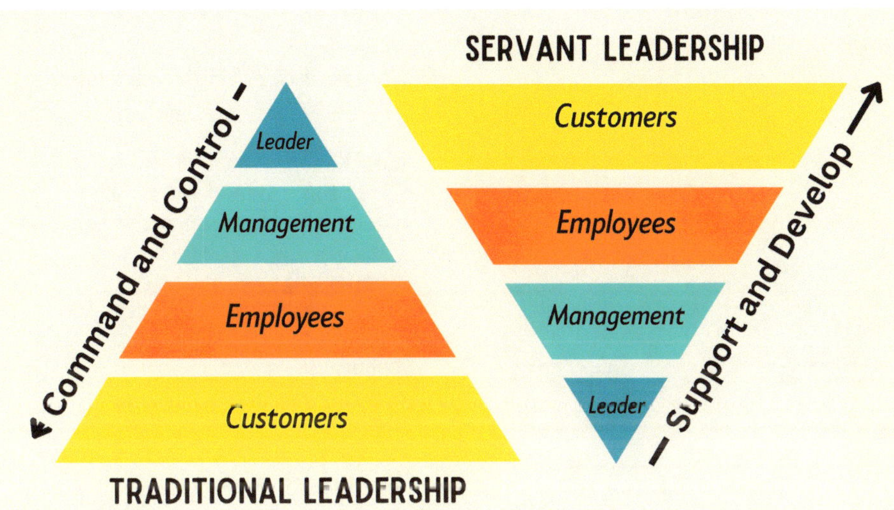

How it works

Servant leadership differs from traditional leadership in its focus and approach.

While traditional leaders often prioritize their own authority, servant leaders prioritize serving the needs of their team members and the customers.

Traditional leadership may involve a top-down approach with clear hierarchies, while servant leadership emphasizes collaboration and empowerment. Servant leaders listen actively, empathize with their team, and prioritize their development.

Applying Servant Leadership

You can apply Servant Leadership by:

- Putting customers ahead of everyone else. You can listen to your customer's feedback, and align your roadmaps and priorities accordingly
- Coaching and developing your employees, and being empathetic to their concerns and challenges. This means setting up a culture that is inclusive, and employee friendly
- Promoting a non-authoritative, inclusive approach to decision making.

Situational Leadership

Paul Hersey, Ken Blanchard (*"Management of Organizational Behavior"*)

Situational leadership enables leaders to adapt their leadership style to fit the specific needs and circumstances of their team and tasks. This flexibility allows leaders to effectively guide their team towards success in various situations.

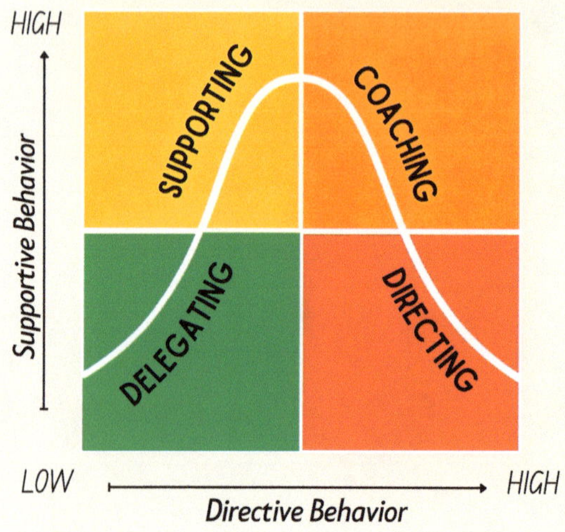

Directing
"Leader decides": High directive and low supportive behavior.

Coaching
"Let's talk, leader decides": High directive and high supportive behavior

Supporting
"Let's talk, employee decides": Low directive and high supportive behavior.

Delegating
"Employee decides": Low directive and low supportive behavior

How it works

Situational leadership involves assessing the readiness and capabilities of team members.

Leaders adjust their leadership style based on the situation and the developmental level of individuals.

They may adopt a directive approach for inexperienced members and a more participative style for those with higher competence.

Flexibility is key; leaders must continuously monitor progress and adapt their approach accordingly.

Applying Situational Leadership

You can apply situational leadership by:

- Assessing your team members' readiness and capabilities.
- Adapting your leadership style based on situation and individual developmental levels.
- Tailoring leadership approach based on evolving team needs and tasks. For example, you may provide hands-on guidance to a new team member while allowing a seasoned employee more independence in project management.

Chapter 21

Leadership Development

*"A sign of a good leader is not how many followers you have
but how many leaders you create."*
Mahatma Gandhi

The Leadership Grid

Robert Blake and Jane Mouton

The Leadership Grid provides a framework for understanding and improving leadership effectiveness by emphasizing the balance between *concern for people* and *concern for production*, facilitating better decision-making and team management.

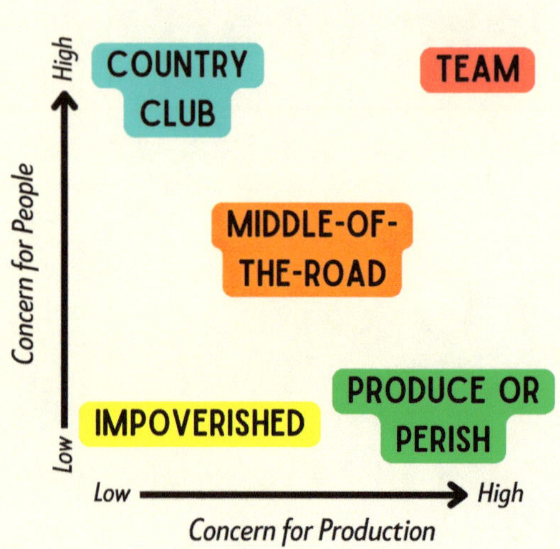

Country Club Management
Thoughtful attention to people, but less challenging

Impoverished Management
Ignoring that the people exist

Product or Perish Management
Getting the work done no matter how the people feel

Team Management
Keeping people challenged and supported at the same time

Middle-of-the-road Management
Balancing morale and results

How it works

The Blake Mouton Leadership Grid assesses leadership styles based on two dimensions: *concern for people* and *concern for production*.

Leaders' behaviors are plotted on a grid, with varying levels of emphasis on each dimension.

Depending on where the behaviors are plotted, the grid identifies five leadership styles: *impoverished, country club, produce or perish, middle-of-the-road*, and *team*. These are then used to assess where the leader needs to focus his/her attention.

Applying the Leadership Grid

You can apply the Blake Mouton Leadership Grid by:

- Assessing your leadership style using the grid's dimensions.
- Striving to balance concern for people and concern for production.
- Tailoring your leadership approach based on situational needs.
- Investing your time in team-building activities to enhance interpersonal relationships.
- Providing clear expectations to your team while offering support and recognition.

McKinsey 9-box Model

McKinsey & Company

The McKinsey 9-Box Model enables systematic talent assessment, succession planning, and development strategies, facilitating informed decisions to identify and nurture high-potential leaders within organizations.

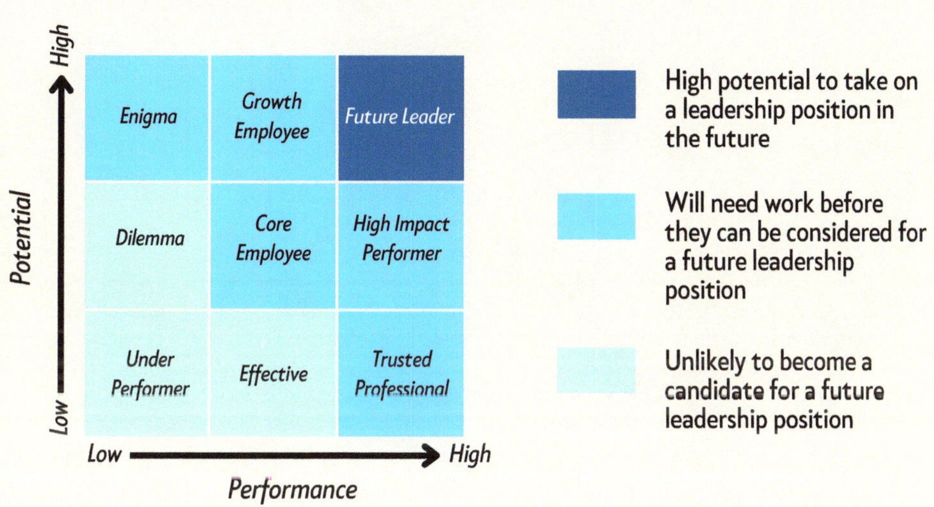

How it works

The McKinsey 9-Box Model assesses leaders based on two dimensions: *performance* and *potential*.

Leaders are plotted on a grid with nine boxes, each representing a combination of performance and potential levels.

This model helps identify high-potential leaders for development opportunities, succession planning, and strategic talent management.

You can use the 9-box grid to allocate resources effectively and prepare a pipeline of future leaders.

Applying the 9-box Model

You can apply the McKinsey 9-Box Model by:

- Conducting regular talent assessments
- Evaluating leaders based on performance and potential.
- Identifying high-potential individuals for leadership development programs.
- Implementing succession plans by grooming identified successors for key roles.
- Providing targeted coaching and mentorship to individuals